PENGUIN

D0644641

BRAND

HENRIK IBSEN was born at Skien, Norway, in 1828. His family went bankrupt when he was a child, and he struggled with poverty for many years. His first ambition was medicine, but he abandoned this to write and to work in the theatre. Of his early verse plays, *The Vikings at Helgeland* is now best remembered. In the year of its publication, 1858, he married Susannah Thoresen, a pastor's daughter.

A scholarship enabled Ibsen to travel to Rome in 1864. In Italy he wrote *Brand* (1866), which earned him a state pension, and *Peer Gynt* (1867), for which Grieg later wrote the incidental music. These plays established his reputation. Apart from two short visits to Norway, he lived in Italy and Germany until 1891.

From *The League of Youth* (1869) onwards, Ibsen renounced poetry and wrote prose drama. Though a timid man, he supported in his plays many crucial causes of his day, such as the emancipation of women. Plays like *A Doll's House* (1879) and *Ghosts* (1881) caused a critical uproar. Other plays include *The Pillars of the Community*, *The Wild Duck*, *The Lady from the Sea*, *Hedda Gabler*, *The Master Builder*, *John Gabriel Borkmann* and *When We Dead Wake*.

Towards the end of his life Ibsen, one of the world's greatest dramatists, suffered strokes which destroyed his memory for words and even for the alphabet. He died in 1906 in Kristiania (now Oslo).

GEOFFREY HILL was born in 1932 at Bromsgrove, Worcestershire, where his father was a police constable. He attended Fairfield village school, the County High School, Bromsgrove, and Keble College, Oxford (which elected him to an honorary fellowship in 1981). He taught for many years at Leeds University and later at Cambridge, where he is an Honorary Fellow of Emmanuel College. In 1988 he moved to the USA and he is now a member of the University Professors Program at Boston University. He is the author of five books of poetry and two collections of critical essays; his *Collected Poems* is published in the Penguin International Poets series. His version of Ibsen's *Brand* was produced at the National Theatre in 1978.

HENRIK IBSEN

BRAND

A version for the stage by
GEOFFREY HILL

PENGUIN BOOKS

PENGUIN BOOKS

Published by the Penguin Group
Penguin Books Ltd, 27 Wrights Lane, London w8 5tz, England
Penguin Books USA Inc., 375 Hudson Street, New York, New York 10014, USA
Penguin Books Australia Ltd, Ringwood, Victoria, Australia
Penguin Books Canada Ltd, 10 Alcorn Avenue, Toronto, Ontario, Canada m4v 3b2
Penguin Books (NZ) Ltd, 182–190 Wairau Road, Auckland 10, New Zealand

Penguin Books Ltd, Registered Offices: Harmondsworth, Middlesex, England

First edition published by Heinemann 1978
Second edition published by the University of Minnesota Press 1981
This edition published in Penguin Books 1996
1 3 5 7 9 10 8 6 4 2

Set in 10/12 pt Monotype Bembo
Typeset by Datix International Limited, Bungay, Suffolk
Printed in England by Clays Ltd, St Ives plc

CONTENTS

PREFACE TO THE
PENGUIN EDITION[1]

This work makes no claim to be a translation of *Brand*. It is a version
for the stage of a poetic drama, or dramatic poem, which was perhaps
not intended for the stage. It is based on an annotated literal prose
translation by Inga-Stina Ewbank, who is not responsible for the liber-
ties I have taken or for errors I may have introduced. My version was
commissioned by the National Theatre, London, and received its first
performance there in April 1978. A first edition was published by
Heinemann in the UK, in 1978, and a second, in the USA, by the
University of Minnesota Press, in 1981.

Although the version runs to more than five thousand lines, it is still
not a complete rendering of Ibsen's text. Those who are able to com-
pare my words with the original Norwegian will detect many in-
stances where lines, and indeed whole passages, have been omitted,
amplified or transposed.

Ibsen composed *Brand* in four-beat verse, sometimes iambic, at
other times trochaic. His rhyme-scheme ranges from the couplet to a
complicated interweaving of rhymes. My version is written largely in
three-beat verse but this is frequently varied with two- and four-beat
verse.

Like Ibsen's, my rhyme-scheme ranges from couplets to more freely
interwoven patterns but I have not tried to follow the threads in his
texture. I have rung the changes in metre and rhyme to achieve variety
of pace and tone in the English verse and have worked by intuition
rather than by textual precedent.

When *Brand* first appeared, in March 1866, from a Copenhagen
publishing house, it brought unchallengeably to an end a long period
of failure and neglect which must, to Ibsen, have seemed interminable.
His status among the Scandinavian intelligentsia as poetic celebrity
was immediately assured. Although most if not all that is overtly

'philosophical' or 'ethical' in the work has evanesced, with much else of that particular *Zeitgeist*, it was none the less upon such intellectual and emotional material that Ibsen's creative energy was greatly exercised and for that reason it remains material to our comprehension.

The strongest thread which drew me – dismayed and exhausted in anticipation – to undertake the present version of *Brand* was itself technical rather than ethical – a remark attributed by William Archer to Ibsen: 'I wanted a metre in which I could career where I would, as on horseback.'[2] I studied, in the light of this observation, the earlier verse translations by F. E. Garrett and C. H. Herford, and came away from that reading properly chastened, but could not see anywhere in their competent and faithful verse that embodiment of poetic energy, at once headstrong and strongly reined, which Michael Meyer has well described as Ibsen's 'marvellous flexibility, moving without incongruity between colloquialism and high poetry'.[3]

In so far as Ibsen succeeded in mastering this element, he also deepened and widened the rift between the metrical, grammatical inexorability of such poetry and the 'inevitability', the 'cosmic' determinism, of such post-Hegelian philosophy as that of Hebbel, by which he may have been influenced either directly or indirectly (though J. W. McFarlane warns us not to make too much of the suggested connection).[4] This notion of a 'rift' is adumbrated in McFarlane's observation that 'in its origins, *Brand* was . . . compounded of distaste, guilt, contempt, and frustration,'[5] and also in Ibsen's own retrospective: 'I would have been quite capable of making the same syllogism just as well about a sculptor or a politician as about a priest.'[6] Ibsen, to my mind, here enjoys a self-made latitude verging on licence, demonstrating one of many ways in which an aggressively iron will to resist may be quietly reconciled with options and conditions. To the extent that *Brand* is compounded of distaste, guilt, contempt, and frustration, we are fortunate. We seem invited to consider it as tragic moral education on a high plane but at this level we might just as well be admiring the loftiness of Tennyson's *Idylls of the King*, Whittier's *The Brewing of Soma* or Longfellow's 'Excelsior'. Ibsen's poetry is ambiguously empowered; *Brand* as 'symbolic project'[7] is, as much as is its eponymous hero, 'uncompromising' yet compromised. A consequence of this discrepancy is that the self-discoveries of the tragic characters Brand and Agnes appear not so much belated as redundant in face of those discoveries of impetus and inertia made within the medium of language itself.

Whereas Brand is a visionary thinker according to nineteenth-century notions of Visionary Thought, Brand's Mother, the Mayor, the Dean, the various representatives of the People, are characterized by a low wariness that is also unawareness. They are carriers of distaste, guilt, contempt and frustration which are at once Ibsen's and their own. McFarlane rightly says that whereas the public figures 'did not require the invention of a Brand for denunciation to work', his character acts as a judge in the condemnation of Einar and his own mother.[8] That he is so uncompromising and yet so available, as foil or reactive agent, is a technical economy which may exact its own price: compromising both his proper availability, his power of priestly mediation, and his more contentious mediations of visionary certitude. By contrast the secondary characters draw more directly from Ibsen's embroilment in a timeless human force which produces and reproduces itself with undiminished vigour from the York *Crucifixion* to the plays of Beckett. They stand, even in their private exposure, for the 'public Opinion', 'vulgar Opinion', as strong as it is inert, which satirists have reviled and rejoiced in for several centuries and which is the common ground of farce and tragedy. Samuel Butler, the seventeenth-century author of the burlesque satire *Hudibras*, declared, 'So much Power has Malice above all other Passions, to highten Wit and Fancy, for malice is Restles, and never finde's ease untill it has vented it self.'[9] Butler's conceit of 'venting' strikingly anticipates Ibsen's own: 'While I was writing *Brand* I had standing on my desk an empty beer glass with a scorpion in it. From time to time the creature became sickly; then I used to throw a piece of soft fruit to it, which it would then furiously attack and empty its poison into; then it grew well again. Is there not something similar to that about us poets?'[10]

There is a compelling half-truth in Pound's adage that 'a great deal of literature is born of hate'. Is it also to be said of *Brand*, as Pound said of such literature, that 'whatever is sound in it emerges from the ruins'?[11] Is *Brand* a 'ruined' tragedy or a 'sound' tragic farce? I do not think that I have consciously asked myself that question until now. None the less my subconscious mind, or whatever it is that is effective in these matters, must have come to a decision at some point in my two years' labour. Whether or not Ibsen left us a ruined tragedy, my

English version appears to have defined itself as a tragic farce. If it is sound, the soundness will be self-evident within the textures of the verse.

Looking back almost twenty years to the Royal National Theatre production in April 1978, I see it now as having had two large ambitions, neither of which it succeeded in fulfilling. It desired to reinvigorate a wilting conventional idea that poetic tragedy is ineluctably 'Promethean' but also saw in this an opportunity – not to be missed – of demonstrating to the full the newly installed stage-machinery of the Olivier Theatre. The result was a theatrical hybrid in which a psychological pseudo-naturalism, more suited to the tele-vising of Sartre, was made arbitrarily 'poetic' by grandiosity of effects. It must be added, in justice, that I was present at a number of rehearsals and therefore share responsibility for the failure to 'realize' the play.

The entire cast of that production has my respect and gratitude. I trust that, nearly twenty years on, it will not seem either invidious or otiose if I name one performance that remains in the mind, with particular clarity, as having stood fast to the verse-line. I have to dis-sent here from Meyer's implied preference for performances where one 'almost forgets that rhyme is being used'.[12] In *Brand* the audience should not forget for a moment that the dramatic medium is rhymed verse. I cite the exemplary instance of Patience Collier as Brand's Mother, the slightest movement of tightening lip or knuckle perfectly read from the metre and syntax.

When I began work on the play I believe I said to myself, if a metre in which to career 'as on horseback' is what Ibsen desires, he shall have it – in English. If I have succeeded, or at least come close to success, in fulfilling my intention, there will be no need for either director or actors to project feeling, empathy, into the verse; it will not be neces-sary for anyone to practise getting 'inside' a character; no one will need to do background research. The verse itself is at once character and enactment; is itself both absolute will and contingency. The play can therefore move forward as swiftly as the essential requirement of accurate verse-speaking will permit.

Massive and elaborate stage-machinery may also be dispensed with. I can envisage a heroic performance of this version in a puppet-theatre, always provided that those responsible for speaking the verse follow the tradition and discipline to which I have here paid tribute.

It remains for me to add that, in preparing this third edition for the press, I have made a considerable number of further word-changes, including deletions and additions, throughout the play.

NOTES

1 The first four paragraphs of this Preface incorporate, with slight changes of wording, the 'Note on the Text' from the first edition (Heinemann, 1978).

2 'Ibsen As I Knew Him', quoted in Michael Meyer, *Ibsen: A Biography* (Doubleday, 1971), 245. This is an appropriate point at which to pay tribute to the exemplary technical detailing of Inga-Stina Ewbank's commentary and annotations which were in themselves an inspiration and a sustaining force. For two years I enjoyed privileged access to an unpublished work of translation and scholarship magisterial in its cogency of knowledge and insight. I also recall with gratitude an *aperçu* from Sir Peter Hall. At our earliest conference, we were discussing metre and I observed that I would have to resist the pull of the English dramatic pentameter against *Brand*'s tetrameter. He agreed, adding, 'Why not try something even shorter than tetrameter?' The best gifts one person can make to another, in this field of endeavour, are technical details; it is the precise detail, of word or rhythm, which carries the ethical burden; it is technique, rightly understood, which provides the true point of departure for inspiration.

3 *ibid.*

4 *The Oxford Ibsen*, vol. III (Oxford University Press, 1972), 31–3. This and the following extracts are quoted by kind permission of Oxford University Press.

5 *ibid.*, 1.

6 *ibid.*, 441: Ibsen, letter of 26 June 1869, to Georg Brandes.

7 *ibid.*, 19. McFarlane applies this term to Brand's rebuilding of the church.

8 *ibid.*, 15: '*agent provocateur*' is McFarlane's term for Brand's role in relation to the public figures.

9 Samuel Butler, *Prose Observations*, ed. H. De Quehen (Clarendon Press, 1979), 60. Quoted by kind permission of Oxford University Press.

10 *The Oxford Ibsen*, III, 443: letter of 29 October 1870, to Peter Hansen.

11 D. Anderson, 'Breaking the Silence: The Interview of Vanni Ronsisvalle and Pier Paolo Pasolini with Ezra Pound in 1968', *Paideuma*, 10 (1981), 336. Quoted by kind permission of the National Poetry Foundation, University of Maine.

12 Henrik Ibsen, *Brand*, translated from the Norwegian by Michael Meyer (Doubleday, 1960), 'Note on the Text', 41. Quoted by kind permission of Michael Meyer and Methuen.

BRAND

A version for the stage

CHARACTERS

BRAND

PEASANT

PEASANT'S SON

EINAR

AGNES

GERD

STARVING MAN

MAYOR

SCRIVENER

NILS SNEMYR

WOMEN OF THE VILLAGE

MEN OF THE VILLAGE

DISTRESSED WOMAN

BOAT OWNER

PEASANTS' SPOKESMAN

BRAND'S MOTHER

DOCTOR

MESSENGER

SECOND MESSENGER

MAN WHO BRINGS WARNING

GYPSY WOMAN

SCHOOLMASTER

SEXTON

DEAN

OFFICIAL

CLERIC

CHORUS OF SPIRITS

ACT ONE

In the snow, high up in the mountains. The mist lies thick; rain and semi-darkness. BRAND, *dressed in black, with a staff and a pack, is slowly making his way westward. A* PEASANT *and his half-grown* SON, *who have joined him, are a little way behind.*

PEASANT [*calling after* BRAND]:
    Hey, Stranger, not so fast!
    Where are you?
BRAND: Here.
PEASANT: We're lost;
    it's never been so thick.
BRAND: We've lost sight of the track.
SON: Hey, look, look, a great split
    in the ice.
PEASANT: Stay clear of it
    for God's sake!
BRAND: I can hear
    a cataract. That roar,
    where is it?
PEASANT: That's the beck
    brasting through ice and rock;
    the devil knows how deep.
    You will, with one more step.
BRAND: I am a priest; I said
    no faltering.
PEASANT: Ay, so you did.
    And I say it's beyond
    all mortal strength. The ground –
    hollow – d'you feel it quake?

Don't tempt your luck. Turn back!

BRAND: This is my destined road.

PEASANT: Ay, and who said so?

BRAND: God
     said so; the God I serve.

PEASANT: Man-of-God, you've got nerve.
     But just heed what I say!
     Though you're bishop or dean,
     or some such holy man,
     you'll be dead before day.
     I can't see past my nose!
     It's miles to the next house,
     I know that for a fact.
     Don't be so stiff-necked.
     You've only got the one
     life, and when that's gone . . .

BRAND: If we can't see the way
     we'll not be led astray
     by marsh light or false track.

PEASANT: There's ice tarns, worse than t'beck;
     they'll be the death of us.

BRAND: Not so! We'll walk across.

PEASANT: Walk on the water?

BRAND: He
     walked on Lake Galilee.

PEASANT: A good few years ago
     that was. It's harder now.
     Try if you must, go on;
     but you'll sink like a stone!

BRAND: I owe God life and death.
     He's welcome to them both.

PEASANT: You're worse than lost, you're mad!

BRAND [stopping, then coming nearer again]:
     But lately, man-of-earth,
     you thought this journey worth
     the risk. 'Come ice, come snow,'
     you said; and told me how
     your lass, down at the fjord,

4

    lies at death's door.

PEASANT: Afeard,
  'less she bids me farewell,
  Old Nick will grab her soul.

BRAND: You must get there today;
  you said so.

PEASANT: I did, ay!

BRAND: What would you sacrifice
  that she might die in peace?

PEASANT: To keep her soul from harm
  I'd barter house and home;
  I'd give all that I have.

BRAND: 'All', you say. Would you give
  your life?

PEASANT [*scratching his ear*]:
          Life? Now wait,
  now that's asking a lot,
  Christ it is! There's my wife,
    [*Points to* SON]
  and him.

BRAND: Christ gave His life.
  Christ's mother gave her son.

PEASANT: Maybe. Those days are gone,
  and so are miracles.
  It's different nowawhiles.

BRAND: Go! you know not the Lord,
  nor He you!

PEASANT: Agh, you're hard!

SON [*tugging at him*]:
  Come home, let's be gone!

PEASANT: We will that! And you, man-
  of-God!

BRAND: If I refuse?

PEASANT: Stranger, think on! Suppose
  we go and leave you here;
  suppose you disappear
  in a snow drift or get drowned,
  suppose word gets around.

I'd soon be up in court
accused of God knows what.

BRAND: A martyr in His cause.

PEASANT: And that's not worth a curse —
I'm done with God and you!

SON [*screaming, as a hollow rumbling is heard in the distance*]:
An ice-fall!

BRAND [*to the* PEASANT, *who has seized his collar*]:
You! Let go!

PEASANT [*wrestling with* BRAND]:
Not I!

BRAND: Let go, you fool!
[BRAND *tears himself free and throws the* PEASANT
down in the snow.]

PEASANT: Go to the devil!

BRAND: You'll
go to him. That's your fate,
you can be sure of that!
[*He walks off.*]

PEASANT [*sitting rubbing his arm*]:
That's doing the Lord's work,
is it? He nearly broke
my arm.
[*Shouts after* BRAND *as he gets up*]
Hey, man-of-faith,
help us to find the path!

BRAND: No need. You've found your road:
the way that is called broad.

PEASANT: I pray he's right this time —
God bring us safely home.
[*He and his* SON *walk off in an easterly direction.*]

BRAND [*appears higher up, looking in the direction that the*
PEASANT *took*]:
Crawl off, then, you poor slave!
Drudge where you fear to strive.
When our weak flesh alone
fails us, we struggle on
and on with bleeding feet.

Sheer will-power bears the weight.
Strange how the lifeless cling
to life with 'Life's the thing!'
Small men, who set great store
by life, dread all the more
its vision and its pain.
How can you save such men,
who talk of 'sacrifice'
yet barter truth for peace?
    [*Smiles as if remembering something*]
When I was just a boy
daydreaming at school,
I thought, 'Suppose an owl
were frightened of the dark.'
I laughed behind my book.
Many and many a day
the teacher had me out.
'And there's a fish,' I thought,
'somewhere, that hates the sea.'
As the taws cracked, I grinned;
those two thoughts gripped my mind.
I gazed across a gulf
dividing those who dare
from those who fear to be.
Too many souls are still
like that fish, or that owl:
with their true life to make
in the depths of the dark,
if they could but endure;
who flee from their dark star,
each from his own true self;
perish in this world's air.
    [*Stops for a moment, notices something, and listens*]
Yet, for a moment, there is song
in the air; and laughter among
the singing; and the sound of cheers.
The sun rises and the mist is thin
already; and the plains begin

to glitter. I see travellers
clearly outlined along the crest
of the near ridge; signs of farewell,
handclasps and kisses, a lifted veil,
two youngsters parting from the rest.
They race towards me hand in hand
across the moorland, like brother
and sister, through vivid heather.
Light as a feather she skims the ground;
and he is lithe, like a young birch.
They play a childish game of catch
and all of life becomes a game.
Their laughter's like a morning hymn.

> [EINAR *and* AGNES, *clad in light travelling clothes,
> both of them warm and glowing, come across the plateau,
> as if in the midst of a game. The mist is gone; it is a
> clear summer morning in the mountains.*]

EINAR: Butterfly, butterfly,
Where are you flying?
AGNES: Far far away
From your cruel sighing.
EINAR: Butterfly, butterfly,
Rest from your dance.
You're all of a flutter.
AGNES: Why
All this pretence?
EINAR: Butterfly, butterfly,
Lie in my hand.
AGNES: If I do I shall die.
Let me go on the wind.

> [*Without noticing, they have come to a precipice; they
> are now on the edge of it.*]

BRAND [*crying out to them from above*]:
Stop! Stop, you foolish pair!
EINAR: Who's that?
AGNES [*pointing upward*]:
                    Look! Up there!
BRAND: That cliff – it's undermined! –

beneath you – can't you understand? –
You are both dancing on thin air!

EINAR [*putting his arm around* AGNES *and laughing as he looks
towards* BRAND]:
Agnes and I don't have a care.

AGNES: Old age is time enough for fears.

EINAR: Our youth shall last a hundred years.

BRAND: I see. A summer of sweet mirth,
young butterflies. Then back to earth.

AGNES [*swinging her veil*]:
No, not to earth. My love and I
are wandering children of the sky.

EINAR: A hundred years, in this bright world,
of never really growing old.
Time on our side, all time a game . . .

BRAND: And then?

EINAR: Restored to Heaven and home!

BRAND: You seem so very sure.

EINAR: O yes,
Heaven's our permanent address!

AGNES: Einar, Einar! He knows we came
over the ridge. Stop teasing him!

EINAR: We've said our fond farewell to friends,
kissed and embraced and shaken hands
and made all sorts of promises.
Don't stand there like a troll of ice!
Come down, and let me thaw you out
with wonders that will melt your heart.
Be moved, man, by the power of joy;
don't cast a gloom across our day.
My tale begins. As you perceive,
I am an artist. I can give
wings to my thoughts, and charm all life
to radiance: a flower, a wife.
I take creation in my stride,
as I chose Agnes for my bride
that day I strode up from the South . . .

AGNES: The spirit of eternal youth!

His confidence was like a king's
and he could sing a thousand songs.

EINAR: A thousand? Yes! Some inner voice
kept whispering, 'Your masterpiece
awaits you. Seek her where she dwells
beside the streams, on the high fells!'
And so I sought, up through the woods
of conifers and where the clouds
fly swiftly under Heaven's vault,
that creature without flaw or fault.
Suddenly, suddenly, she was there:
beauty enough for my desire!

AGNES: Poor simple Agnes neatly caught,
a butterfly in passion's net.

EINAR: Oh, nothing ventured, nothing won!
Formalities must wait their turn.
But their turn came; and the guests came;
and there was feasting at the farm,
where blessings sought and blessings given
made the old rafters ring to Heaven.
Three days and nights of feast and song!
And, when we left, that loving throng
followed and cheered us on our way
and were true celebrants of joy.
We drank the wine of fellowship
together from a silver cup.

AGNES: All through the summer night . . .

EINAR: The mist
parted before us, where we passed.

BRAND: And now you go . . . ?

EINAR: On to the town,
our wedding and our honeymoon.
We'll sail away, two swans in flight,
far to the South!

BRAND: And after that?

EINAR: A legend! An unbroken dream
made safe from sorrow, as from time.
There, on the height, without a priest

in sight to bless us, we were blest.

BRAND: Oh, indeed. Who blessed you then?

EINAR: Our friends, with love; as you'll have seen,
this very morning on the ridge.
In parting, we received their pledge
that every dark word, every dark
thought, that could raise a storm or lurk
in the bright foliage of a bower,
is banished from love's book-of-prayer.
Even such words as bear a shade
of darker meaning, they forbade.
They named us the true heirs of joy.

BRAND: So be it then.

>   [*He prepares to leave.*]

EINAR [*taken aback and looking more closely at* BRAND]:

>   I say . . .

I remember that face!
Surely I recognize . . .

BRAND [*coldly*]:

>   A man you never met . . .

EINAR: Impossible to forget . . .

BRAND: I was your childhood friend
but we are men now.

EINAR: Brand,
it's you! So I was right!

BRAND: As soon as I caught sight
of you, I knew you.

EINAR: Still
the same old Brand! At school,
even, you seemed remote,
secure in your own thought.

BRAND: And with good cause. Your calm
South-land was never home
to me. And I felt cold,
shut in that easy world.

EINAR: Is this where you belong?

BRAND: Not now. When I was young
I did. Now I obey

the call, and cannot stay.

EINAR: So you're a man-of-God.

BRAND [*smiling*]:

I have been so described.
I bear the Word, now here
now there. The mountain hare
is more settled than I.
But this is the true way.

EINAR: Where will it end, this true
journey?

BRAND: What's that to you?

EINAR: Brand!

BRAND [*changing his tone*]:

Well, never mind . . .
I'll soon be outward bound
like you . . . on the same boat.

EINAR: Agnes, do you hear that?
Brand's journey is the same
as ours!

BRAND: Fondle your dream,
Einar. The place I seek,
if you came near, could turn
your wedding to a wake,
your dancers into stone.
I seek the death of God,
that dying God of yours
dying these thousand years.
I'll see him in his shroud.

AGNES: Einar, we should go.

EINAR: Wait,
Agnes, wait a while.
[*To* BRAND]
What
madness! You must be ill!

BRAND: Sanity's what you call
sickness, I suppose.
A generation whose
pastimes are its care

has sunk almost past cure.
You flirt and play the fool
and leave the bitter toil
to that poor Holy One
sweating blood to atone,
your dear Christ hurt with thorns,
the saviour of your dance.
Dance on, dance to the end,
dance yourselves deaf and blind!

EINAR: You're good at breathing fire,
a real hot-gospeller;
that fear-and-trembling school
has taught you very well!

BRAND: Einar, I leave the new
fashions in faith to you.
I've not come here to preach
for any sect or church.
Not as a formal Christian
even, but as my own man,
I tell you this: I know
the nature of the flaw
that has so thinned and drained
the spirit of our land.

EINAR [*smiling*]:
We're not the kind to drink
deep of life's cup, you think?

BRAND: No. If only you would,
high-stepping meek-and-mild!
Sin if you dare, but have the grace,
at least, to be fulfilled in vice.
At least live up to what you claim;
don't water your good wine with shame!
Among our people I observe
such littleness and loss of nerve.
A little show of holiness
strictly reserved for Sunday use;
little charity, but much talk
of simple, plain, God-fearing folk.

A middling this, a middling that,
never humble, never great.
Above the worst, beneath the best,
each virtue vicious to the rest.

EINAR: Bravo, Brand! Have your say,
just as you will. I'll play
'Amen' in the right place:
I'm quite ready to please.
I'm wholly unperturbed;
my God is still my God.

BRAND: Indeed He's yours! You've even
been favoured by Heaven
with that vision of Him –
it brought you some small fame –
the picture that you did
of your old, pampered God:
white-haired, moist-eyed with age,
his comic turns of rage
send children off to bed
giggling and half-afraid.

EINAR [angry]:
This is . . .

BRAND: 'No joke', you'd say?
Do you want sympathy?
You trim off life from faith,
haver from birth to death,
self-seekers who refuse
man's true way-of-the-Cross
which is: wholly to be
the all-enduring 'I'.
My God is the great god of storm,
absolute arbiter of doom,
imperious in His love!
He is the voice that Moses heard,
He is the pillar of the cloud,
His is the hand that stayed the sun
for Joshua in Gibeon.
Your God can hardly move;

he's weak of mind and heart,
easy to push about.
But mine is young: a Hercules,
not fourscore of infirmities.
Though you may smile and preen,
Einar; though you bow down
to your own brazenness,
I shall heal this disease
that withers heart and brain,
and make you all new men!

EINAR [*shakes his head*]:
You'll blow the old lamps out
before new lamps are lit;
abandon the known word
for speech as yet unheard.

BRAND: Why must you misconstrue
so much? I seek for nothing new.
I know my mission: to uphold
truths long forgotten by the world;
eternal truths. I have not come
to preach dogmatics or proclaim
the right of some exclusive sect
to rule through pain of interdict.
For every church and creed
is something that this world has made;
and everything that's made must end.
I speak of what endures,
of what is lost and found
eternally. Faith did not climb
slowly from the primeval slime,
nor burst from the volcanic fires.
It is incarnate through recourse
of spirit to our spirit's source.
Though hucksters in and out of church
make tawdry everything they touch,
hawking the relics of their trade,
their bits of dogma, parts
of broken creeds and hearts,

that spirit shines amid the void,
amid the travesties
of things that are, the truth that is.
And, truth-begotten, God's true heir,
the new Adam . . .

EINAR: We should part here,
I think. It's for the best.

BRAND: Here are two paths: the west
for you; for me the north.
Different ways, yet both
end at the fjord. Farewell,
butterflies!

          [*Turning as he starts the descent*]
               Learn to tell
true from false. Don't forget
life's the real work of art!

EINAR [*waving him away*]:
Though you may shake my world
my God stands firm!

BRAND: He's old,
Einar; don't worry Him.
Leave me to bury Him!

          [*He goes down the path.* EINAR *goes silently over and
          looks down after* BRAND. AGNES *stands for a moment
          as if lost in thought; then she starts, looks about her
          uneasily.*]

AGNES: It's all so gloomy. Where's the sun?

EINAR: Behind that cloud, there. Things will soon
look bright again.

AGNES: And there's a fierce
wind out of nowhere. It's like ice.

EINAR: Some freak gust hurtling through the pass,
I'd say. It's much too cold for us
to linger here. Come on!

AGNES: How black
and forbidding that great south peak
seems now. It wasn't always so,
surely?

EINAR: You've let Brand frighten you
    with his dour face and talk of doom.
    Look here, I'll race you! You'll get warm!
AGNES: I can't. I'm tired.
EINAR: To tell the truth,
    love, so am I. This downhill path
    is tricky too. But we'll be safe
    on *terra firma* soon enough.
    And, Agnes, now the sun's come back
    the world no longer looks so bleak.
    What a picture! Such harmony
    of sky with sea and sea with sky;
    deep azure lit by silver streaks,
    suffused with golden lights and darks,
    out to the far horizon's edge,
    the boundless main! And, look, that smudge
    of smoke – the steamer coming in,
    the very ship we go to join.
    By early evening we shall be
    clear of this place, well out to sea.
    We'll dance on deck and sing; our games
    will make Brand giddy if he comes.
AGNES [*without looking at him and in a hushed voice*]:
    Tell me, are we awake,
    Einar? When that man spoke
    he burned! It seemed each feature
    changed! He grew in stature!
         [*She goes down the path.* EINAR *follows.*]

★

A path along the mountain wall with a wild valley on the right-hand side.
Above and behind the mountain one can see glimpses of greater heights with
peaks and snow. BRAND *appears high up on the path, starts to descend, stops*
midway on a rock which juts out, and looks down into the valley.

BRAND: Now I see where I am:
    strangely close to home.
    Everything I recall

from childhood here still
but smaller now and much
shabbier; and the church
looks in need of repair.
The cliffs loom; the glacier
juts and hangs: it is an
ice wall concealing the sun.
And for all their rough gleam
the fjord waters look grim
and menacing. A small
boat pitches in a squall.
Down there's the timber wharf
and nearby – iron-red roof,
red-flaking walls – the house
to which I would refuse
the name 'home' if I could;
the place where I endured
harsh kinship, an alien
life that was called mine.
Solitude and desire
magnified what was there.
As though in recompense
to my own soul, a sense
of greatness visited me,
made even a poverty-
stricken smallholding shine,
a visionary demesne.
All that has faded. Now
there is nothing to show
what my child-soul once made
out of such solitude.
Returning, I am shorn
of all strength: Samson
in the harlot's lap.

    [Looks again down into the abyss]
It seems they have woken up.
Men, women, children come
from the cottages, climb

slowly among the outcrops
of rock, the lowest slopes;
now lost from sight and now
seen again, on the brow
by the church. Slaves to both
day labour and the sloth
of their own souls; their need
crawls and is not heard
in the courts of Heaven;
and their prayers are craven:
'Give us bread! give us bread!'
So they still eat their God.
Nothing else matters
to them: tossed on storm waters
of the age, the merest flotsam,
or rotting in a foul calm.

> [BRAND *is about to go; a stone is thrown from above
> and rolls down the slope just missing him.* GERD, *a
> fifteen-year-old girl, runs along the ridge with stones in
> her apron.*]

GERD: Hey! Now he's really wild!

BRAND: Who's there? Ah – stupid child!

GERD: Look, he's not a bit hurt,
though I'm sure he was hit.

> [*Throws more stones and cries out*]

Oh . . . he's back . . . swooping down
at me . . . his claws . . . I'm all torn!

BRAND: Tell me, in God's name, what . . .

GERD: Stay there and keep quiet
if you want to be safe.
It's all right, he's flown off.

BRAND: Who has flown off?

GERD: You
didn't see the hawk?

BRAND: No.

GERD: Not that great ugly thing
with some sort of red ring
round his eye?

BRAND: I did not.

GERD: And with his crest all flat
    against his head?

BRAND: No. Which
    way are you going?

GERD: To church.

BRAND: But the church is down there.

GERD [*looking at him with a scornful smile and pointing
        downward*]:
    Not that one. That's a poor
    tumbledown little place.

BRAND: You know a better?

GERD: Yes,
    yes, yes! Follow me up
    these mountains, to the top.
    That's where my own church is,
    in the heart of the ice.

BRAND: Ah, now I understand.
    I'd forgotten that legend
    of the Ice Church: a great cleft
    in the rock, where the drift-
    ing snow and ice have built
    the roof of a huge vault.
    The church floor is a lake
    frozen as hard as rock,
    so all the stories say.

GERD: Well, they're true!

BRAND: Stay away
    from there. It's sure to fall.
    A gust of wind, a call,
    or a gunshot, could bring
    the end of everything.

GERD [*not listening*]:
    I'll show you where a herd
    of dead reindeer appeared
    out of the glacier last
    spring, when it thawed.

BRAND: You must

never go there. I've told
you why.

GERD [*pointing downward*]:
     That musty old
church of yours! Stay away
from it. I've told *you* why.

BRAND: God bless you. Go in peace.

GERD: Oh, do come! Hear the ice
sing mass, and the wind make
sermons over the rock.
Oh, how you'll burn and freeze!
It's safe from the hawk's eyes.
He settles on Black Peak
just like a weathercock.

BRAND [*aside*]:
Her spirit struggles to be heard;
flawed music from a broken reed.
God in His judgement sometimes draws
evil to good. Not from *these* throws.

GERD: O the hawk, O the whir
of his wings! Help me, sir!
I must hide. In my church
it's safe. Hey! hey! can't catch
me! O but he's angry. Now
what shall I do? I'll throw
things. Ugh! keep off me, keep
off me with those great sharp
claws! Strike me, I'll strike you!
     [*She runs off up the mountain.*]

BRAND: So that's churchgoing too;
those howls are hymns of praise.
But is she worse than those
who seek God in the valley?
And is her church less holy?
Who sees? And who is blind?
Who wanders? Who is found?
Feckless, with his garlands on,
dances till he plunges down

into the terrible abyss.
Dullness mutters 'thus and thus',
his catechism's sleepy rote,
and treads the old, deep-trodden rut.
Madness wanders from itself,
half shadowing the other half;
immortal longings gone astray,
confusing darkness with the day.
My way is clear, now. Heaven calls.
I know my task. When those three trolls
are dead, mankind shall breathe again,
freed from old pestilence and pain.
Arm, arm, my soul! Unsheathe your sword!
Fight now for all true sons of God!

[*He descends into the populated valley.*]

ACT TWO

Down by the fjord with steep mountain walls all round. The old dilapidated church stands on a small knoll nearby. A storm is gathering. The PEASANTS, *men, women and children, are gathered in groups, some on the shore, some on the slopes. The* MAYOR *is sitting in the midst of them on a stone; a* SCRIVENER *is helping him; grain and other provisions are being distributed.* EINAR *and* AGNES *are standing surrounded by a group of people, farther towards the background. A few boats are lying off the shore.* BRAND *appears on the slope by the church without being noticed by the crowd.*

A MAN [*bursting through the crowd*]:
   Let me past! Let me past!
A WOMAN: Hey you, we was first!
MAN [*pushing her aside*]:
   Get out of the way, or . . .
   See to me first, Mayor!
MAYOR: Give me time, give me time . . .
MAN: I must have my share;
   I've bairns back at home,
   starving, all four, five . . .
MAYOR [*jokingly*]:
   You don't sound too sure.
MAN: One was barely alive
   when I left.
MAYOR: Here, hold on,
   have I got your name down?
      [*Leafs through his papers*]
   H'm . . . h'm . . . you're in luck.
   Twenty-nine . . . in the sack.
      [*To the* SCRIVENER]

Whoa there, whoa there,
that's enough, that's his lot.
Nils Snemyr?

SNEMYR: I'm here.

MAYOR: Your ration's been cut.
Well, you've one less to feed.

SNEMYR: My wife, ay, she's dead;
passed on yesterday.

MAYOR: It's an ill wind they say . . .
she'll need no more porridge.

   [*To* SNEMYR *who is leaving*]
Forget about marriage;
just give it a rest.

SCRIVENER: Hee, hee!

MAYOR: What's the joke?

SCRIVENER: Just hearing you talk,
Mr Mayor, it's a treat.

MAYOR: Hold your jaw shut!
I don't find this funny.
But 'laugh or you'll cry',
it's the only way.

EINAR [*coming out of the crowd with* AGNES]:
They've had my last crust,
and my last penny.
Never mind, I can pawn
my watch or my stick
or my haversack.
I'll rake up the fare
for the boat, never fear!

MAYOR: My word, you arrived
not a moment too soon.
These folk are half-starved.
And they're plump and thriving
Compared to the starving!

   [*Catches sight of* BRAND *and points upward*]
Bravo! Welcome, friend!
You've heard, too, no doubt,
of our deluge and drought.

We'll be glad to receive
any gift you can give,
in cash or in kind.
I tell you this parish is
chewing on air.
'We need miracles, Mayor!'
A fat lot of help,
five loaves and three fishes!
They'd go at one gulp!

BRAND: Feed the five thousand in the name
of Mammon and you'd famish them.

MAYOR: Spare us your homilies.
Fine words fill no bellies.

EINAR: Brand, Brand, use your eyes!
Look, famine and disease
all around us. They're
dying by the score.

BRAND: Yes, I can recognize
all the dread signs.
I know the lord who reigns
here, and his tyrannies.

    [*Steps down among the crowd and says emphatically*]
If life were set in its old course,
the old routine of Adam's curse,
spiritless labour, soulless greed,
I might throw you some hunks of bread.
If all a man does is crawl home
each night, dog-tired, let him become
the thing he seems — an animal.
A stifling weariness of days
entombs us in the blank belief
that God has torn our destinies,
our very names, out of the Book of Life.
And yet He is merciful.

VOICES FROM THE CROWD: Argh! Kick us when we're
    down!

MAYOR: Who does he mean, *Mammon*?

BRAND: If I could heal you with my blood

I'd willingly see it poured
out of every vein.
But that would be a sin
against God, and His gift
of suffering. His desire
is to show mercy, to lift
you out of your own mire.
Rejoice in what He gives.
A people that so strives,
though all else has gone,
will be restored to its own.
But when that spirit's dead
it is death indeed.

A WOMAN: A storm, a storm! The fjord's
    lashing out at his words!

ANOTHER WOMAN: He utters blasphemies,
    don't heed what he says!

BRAND: What wonders can *your* God perform?

A THIRD WOMAN: A storm, look, a storm!

VOICES: Stone him! Grr, drive him out!
    Yes. Yes! Grab his coat!

        [*The* PEASANTS *swarm threateningly round* BRAND.
        The MAYOR *intervenes. A* WOMAN, *wild and dishev-*
        elled, comes running down the slope.]

DISTRESSED WOMAN: Help me, for the love of Christ!

MAYOR: I'll do what I can, ma'am,
    provided that your name
    is on our parish list.
    Let me take a look.

DISTRESSED WOMAN: No, no! For pity's sake . . .
    hunger's nothing now.
    I've seen a horror worse
    than you can know!

MAYOR: What d'you mean? Speak up!

DISTRESSED WOMAN: I can't
    tell *you*. It's a priest I want.

MAYOR: There isn't a priest
    in these parts.

DISTRESSED WOMAN: Then I'm lost,
    utterly alone.
BRAND [*approaching*]:
    A priest, you say? There may be one . . .
DISTRESSED WOMAN: Tell him to hurry. Please . . .
BRAND: I must know what's the matter.
    I assure you, the priest will come.
DISTRESSED WOMAN: Across all that wild water?
BRAND: Yes.
DISTRESSED WOMAN: Back there . . . at home . . .
    my husband . . . bairns as well . . .
    Say he won't go to Hell!
BRAND: First you must tell me why
    you've come.
DISTRESSED WOMAN: My breasts were dry,
    and the babe went unfed.
    Folk wouldn't heed, nor God.
    My man couldn't bear it.
    It broke his spirit,
    and he just upped and killed
    it, like that, the child . . .
BRAND: He killed . . .
VOICES [*with dread*]:
                    His child.
DISTRESSED WOMAN: The moment
    it was done, his torment
    was dreadful to see,
    and he wanted to die.
    He turned the knife on him-
    self, and screamed Satan's name.
    He'll not live, but he's afraid
    to go. He lies with the child dead
    and frozen in his arms,
    and cries and blasphemes.
    Come with me, sir. At least
    he'll not go unconfessed.
MAYOR: What's your name?
    [*Points to his papers*]

Is it here?

BRAND [*sharply, to the* PEASANTS]:
Take me across the fjord.

A MAN: In this? We wouldn't dare!

BRAND: A soul facing its doom
can't linger till it's calm.

ANOTHER MAN: The madman's tempting God!

MAYOR: Go the long way round.

DISTRESSED WOMAN: There'd still be the river
to cross; and the bridge's down.
Just after I'd crossed over . . .
it went . . . I might've drowned.

BRAND [*stepping down into a boat and loosening the sail*]:
You! Will you risk your boat?

OWNER: No . . . yes . . .

BRAND: Good, that's a start!
Now, who'll chance his life?

FIRST MAN: I'm staying where it's safe.

DISTRESSED WOMAN: Oh, my man, sir, my man,
he'll die all unshriven,
and shut out of Heaven!

BRAND [*calling from the boat*]:
I need someone to bale
and to trim the sail –
one! No more!
You there, so keen to give
just now! Give all you have!

A VOICE [*threatening*]:
Get back on t'shore.

BRAND [*holding on with the boat hook and shouting*]:
None of you man enough?
Very well, then, a woman . . .
    [*To the* DISTRESSED WOMAN]
You there! Come on, come on!

DISTRESSED WOMAN: Oh, I can't . . . it's so rough . . .
my poor bairns, orphan'd
they'll be if I'm taken . . .
oh . . . oh . . .

BRAND [*laughing*]:
            You built on sand,
poor soul, and your house is shaken
to pieces.

AGNES [*turning, with flaming cheeks, quickly to* EINAR, *and
            putting her hand on his arm*]:
            You heard? Everything?

EINAR: Yes! Admirable! So strong
in his calling!

AGNES: Follow that call!
God bless you, farewell!
        [*Calls out to* BRAND]
Here's one worthy man:
take *him*!

BRAND: · Quickly then!
Here take the rope!

EINAR [*pale*]:
Which one do you mean,
Agnes? Not *me*, surely?

AGNES: I was blind. I see clearly
now. Go, I offer you up.

EINAR: Believe me, I would
have gone; I would! I'd have sailed
joyfully into that storm,
once upon a time.

AGNES [*trembling*]:
But now . . . ?

EINAR: Life is so very sweet,
Agnes. I daren't do it.

AGNES [*shrinking away from him*]:
Einar, what do you mean?

EINAR: I mean . . . I'm afraid.

AGNES: Then you have made
an impassable ocean
rage between us for ever.
        [*To* BRAND]
I'll come with you. Wait!

BRAND: Now or too late!

DISTRESSED WOMAN [*terrified, as* AGNES *leaps on board*]:
Mercy, sweet Saviour!

EINAR: Stay, Agnes, for my sake!

BRAND [*to the* DISTRESSED WOMAN]:
Woman, where do you live?

DISTRESSED WOMAN: Over there. There, d'you see?
Behind the black rock.
[*The boat moves off from the shore.*]

EINAR [*shouting after them*]:
Don't throw your life away,
my dearest! Save yourself, save
yourself. Think of your family!

AGNES: I'm as safe as can be,
Einar. Don't be afraid.
We journey with God.
[*The boat sails off. The* PEASANTS *throng the slopes
and gaze after it in tense excitement.*]

A MAN: There they are, clear of the Point
already!

ANOTHER MAN: No they ain't.

FIRST MAN: They are, they are, you fool.
It's astern and to leeward
I tell you!

A THIRD MAN: See that squall!
Ugh . . . they'll not weather that.

MAYOR: Whoo-oo! there goes his hat!

A WOMAN: Look, his hair, all raven-black,
look how it's blown back.

FIRST MAN: The sea's hissing and boiling
up, like a fountain.

EINAR: What was that? That scream?
I heard it through the storm.

ANOTHER WOMAN: From high on the mountain.

A THIRD WOMAN [*pointing upward*]:
Would you believe . . .? See, Gerd,
Gerd, laughing and howling,
driving the boat on!

FIRST WOMAN: Blowing a ram's horn,

and calling up the fiends
to ride on the winds.

SECOND WOMAN: She's hooting through her hands
now. Drearsome it sounds.

FIRST MAN: Hoot away, you vile troll,
choke on your own spell,
you'll not do them harm.
True faith, that's their shield!

SECOND MAN: With that man at the helm
I'd go as his crew
through a sea twice as wild.

FIRST MAN [to EINAR]:
Who is he, d'you know?

EINAR: Some kind of – priest.

THIRD MAN: Well, one thing's plain.
Priest or not, he's a man.

FIRST MAN: There's our pastor, I say –
our new pastor.

VOICES: Ay!

[*They disperse over the hill slopes.*]

MAYOR: God help us, why such fuss?
The woman's not from here;
and he's not one of us.
Why should he interfere,
rushing off, risking his neck,
and for nothing, so to speak?
Well, I go by the book
in my own bailiwick!

[*Exit.*]

★

Outside the cottage on the headland. It is late in the day. The fjord lies smooth and still. AGNES *is sitting by the shore. Presently* BRAND *comes out of the cottage.*

BRAND: So now it's finished. Death's quiet hand
has smoothed away his grin of dread
and wiped the terror from his mind.

It seems so peaceful to be dead.
He knew as much of his own crime
as his tongue fumbled at to name,
as his stained hands could bear to touch,
as his poor brain could grope to reach.
He knew the half of what he'd done,
mumbling, 'I killed the little one.'
What of the ones he didn't kill
but murdered just the same? Two boys,
staring from the dark ingle-nook,
constrained to look, and look, and look,
with more than terror in their eyes,
not understanding what they saw.
Who can redeem *their* souls from Hell?
What purifying flame shall burn
to ash their memories' carrion?
Condemned to burgeon in the glare
of that one awful, endless sight
like leaves in darkness, sickly-white,
growing more sickly as they grow,
they in their turn shall generate
offspring of their own despair,
scions of wretchedness and hate,
and all the streams of life shall run
from the one ever-spreading stain.
Where did it all begin, and why,
eternal culpability?
What answer blares from the abyss?
'Remember who the father was.'
When the Day of Judgement comes
every soul shall stand accused,
shall be condemned as it condemns,
shall curse, knowing itself accursed.
There'll be no mercy for the plea
'Forgive us our heredity'!
Abysmal riddle, making all
capacities incapable!
Not one soul in a thousand sees

the mountain of offences rise
from the base origins of life,
the two bare, basic words *to live*.

[*A few* PEASANTS *come from behind the cottage and
approach* BRAND.]

SPOKESMAN: So then, we meet again.

BRAND: Why are you here? The man
is dead now; he's no need
of anything you could give.

SPOKESMAN: Not for himself, maybe.
He's with the Lord above.
But what about the three
poor souls he left behind,
and left without a crumb?
We're here because of them . . .
brought them some scraps of food . . .
what bits we could find.

BRAND: Until you hazard all,
the gift's of no avail.

SPOKESMAN: I'll tell you how it is.
If that stranger who lies
in there, all stiff and stark,
had been mid-fjord,
clinging to a rock
or an upturned boat,
I'd have gone to his aid
and hauled him out.
I'd not see him drown.

BRAND: Yet you've little concern
for the death of the soul.

SPOKESMAN: It's scholar's talk, is that.
We're simple folk. We toil
morn to night with our hands,
all the hours that God sends.

BRAND: Then turn your backs on the dawn light.
Gaze at nothing but the ground,
stoop your shoulders to the yoke,
bend your backs until they break.

SPOKESMAN: I expected you'd say,
   'Look up, look up, my friend,
   look up and be free!'
BRAND: Then be free, if you can.
SPOKESMAN: Ay, sir. But teach us how.
   You must lead us.
BRAND: Why?
SPOKESMAN: Many times we've been shown
   the road we should take
   to find our destiny.
   With you it's more than show.
   It is, and that's a fact!
   The truth is, one brave act
   is better than fine talk.
   You're just the man we need
   in this neighbourhood.
BRAND [*uneasy*]:
   What do you need me for?
SPOKESMAN: To be our pastor, sir.
BRAND: Your pastor? I, remain
   here? Impossible, man!
SPOKESMAN: It wasn't always
   like this! In the old days,
   when the harvests were good
   and the cattle well fed,
   and nobody was clemmed
   with hunger, nor numbed
   with cold and despair,
   we had our own priest
   and a church full of prayer.
   But that's in the past.
   These days the sheep starve
   twice over, you might say.
BRAND: Don't ask me to stay.
   Ask anything but that!
   God has called me to serve
   a hungry multitude
   in the world outside.

What could I do here, shut
in by mountain and fjord?
How would I be heard?

SPOKESMAN: Speak out bold and clear
and all the mountains hear
and add their voice to yours,
and then the world hears.

BRAND [*preparing to leave*]:
It's time I set sail.

SPOKESMAN [*barring his way*]:
No, wait! This call, this call
to serve, that you go on
about: it means a lot to you, then?

BRAND: Man! man! It's my whole life!

SPOKESMAN: Then stay. Remember: 'If
you hazard less than all
the gift's of no avail'!

BRAND: No man can give away
his inmost spirit,
that's his for ever,
or hold back, or divert,
the relentless river
of his destiny.

SPOKESMAN: Why, sir, if you drown
destiny in a tarn,
it's not lost, you know!
Come what may,
it'll reach the sea
as rain, or dew.

BRAND [*staring at him*]:
How do you know that?

SPOKESMAN: You taught us it,
when the sea raged,
and the wind surged,
and you went out
and defied death,
put all your faith
in a small boat,

risked life and all
for that poor soul
in there, you shook
our souls awake,
by God you did!
I'd swear we heard
a voice that rang
out clear and strong,
bells on the wind.
You understand . . .
    [*Lowers his voice*]
tomorrow's too late,
tomorrow we'll forget,
tomorrow we'll haul down
the brave flag that's flown
over our heads today.
We'll not glance at the sky.

BRAND [*hard*]:
If you flinch from the call,
and if you won't fight
to be as you ought,
then be honest; remain
earth-bound, grovelling men,
dumb creatures of toil.

SPOKESMAN [*looking at him for a few moments*]:
You've quenched the flame you lit.
God forgive you for that,
and pity us who saw
a great light that's gone now.
    [*He leaves and the others follow silently.*]

BRAND [*gazing after them*]:
One by one, see, one by one,
homeward in a straggling line,
head bowed and shoulders stooped,
half-expecting to be whipped,
as Adam must have looked, when told
to turn his back on Paradise
and go and wander through the world.

Like Adam with his stricken face
staring at nothing, each of them
bears this knowledge for his shame:
blind creatures formed from my desire
to make man new and whole and pure.
Formed and deformed – whose the default?
My masterstroke this thing of guilt!
    [*He is about to leave, but stops as he sees* AGNES *on the*
    shore.]
Has she sat there all this while?
What is it she can hear?
Is it singing in the air?
In the storm, as we drove
on through the wild sea-wave,
she sat, so rapt and still,
wholly without fear,
with the spindrift glistening
upon her brow and hair,
gazing and listening,
yes, listening with her eyes
to secret harmonies!
    [*Approaches her*]
Tell me, what do you stare
at, so intently there?
The fjord winding its way
down to the great sea?

AGNES [*without turning round*]:
Not the fjord; not this earth
even; for both
are veiled from my sight.
Something more great
I glimpse, a world
beautiful to behold,
outlined against the sun.
How all things shine!
Rivers and seas, white peaks,
a glittering wilderness,
with great palm-trees

that sway in the wind,
shadows on bright sand.
It is a world that wakes
yet waits for life. A voice
cries through the emptiness:
'Creator and creature
of your own nature,
Adam, come forth
to life or death!'

BRAND [*rapturously*]:
　　Tell me . . . tell me . . . do you see more?

AGNES [*putting her hand on her breast*]:
　　I feel within me, here
　　in my heart and my soul,
　　the things that I foretell;
　　all births, all destinies.
　　Everything that is
　　awaits its hour,
　　and the time is near.
　　Already, from above,
　　He gazes down
　　with infinite love;
　　and already the crown
　　of infinite sorrow
　　pierces His brow.
　　And a voice cries
　　through the dawn-wilderness:
　　'Creator and creature
　　of your own nature,
　　Adam, come forth
　　to life or death!'

BRAND: The new Adam, yes!
　　We in him, he in us.
　　Truth at the heart's core,
　　our rightful sphere,
　　our destiny, the abode
　　of our selfhood-in-God.
　　There the old vulture

of self-will shall be no more.
I'll let this world
go, self-enthralled,
let it go its way . . .
But if the enemy
strikes at my work,
then I strike back!
I pledge myself to that
truth of the inmost word,
everyman's right
rightly understood,
to be what in truth I am.
      [*Thinks in silence a while*]
But how should that be?
The curse of heredity,
hereditary guilt,
the aboriginal fault,
stakes its own claim.
      [*Stops and looks into the distance*]
Who is this who comes
so slowly; who climbs
with such anguish; who bends,
so, her head; who stands
gasping for breath; who drags
her body in its rags
as if it were a hoard
of precious, secret greed;
who looks like a crow or
hawk nailed to a barn door?
Why is it I feel,
suddenly, a chill
of childish fear,
insidious like hoar frost
here in my breast
as she comes near?
Dear God . . .
      [BRAND'S MOTHER *comes up the slope, stops half*
      visible against the hill, shades her eyes with her hand

and looks around.]

BRAND'S MOTHER: They said I'd find
   him hereabouts. Brand,
   son Brand, you there,
   then? Ugh, this glare
   burns out your eyes.
   That you, son?

BRAND: Yes.

MOTHER: Let's see. Can't hardly tell
   priest from carl
   I'm that mazed. Ay, it's you.

BRAND: Mother, at your house
   I never saw sunrise
   from summer's end till the return
   of the first cuckoo.

MOTHER [*laughing quietly*]:
   Ay, you grow a thick skin
   there: like an icicle-man
   over the waterfall.
   Do what you like,
   skin gets that thick,
   'twill guard your soul.

BRAND: Mother, I can't stay
   any longer.

MOTHER: Ay, ay,
   like when you were a lad,
   always up and about,
   I'll grant you that.
   And you made off
   soon enough!

BRAND: You made sure that I did.

MOTHER: Always had it in mind
   to see you book-learn'd,
   fit for a parson.
   It stood to reason;
   still does.
      [*Looks more closely at him*]
       H'm, but you've grown

some sinew and brawn
on you, no mistake.
You mind you take care,
son. Don't risk your neck!
BRAND: Is that all you can say?
MOTHER: Say more if you know more,
all nice and scholarly.
That madness on the fjord,
d'you think I've not heard?
It's all they talk about
back there, you and that boat.
What happens if you drown,
eh? I'm robbed by my own
son, that's what. Ay, a thief,
that's what you'd be! My life
you're fooling with. I gave
you it, didn't I? I've
got first claim on what's mine.
You're not just flesh and blood.
You're roof-beam, corner-post,
the nails, the wood,
every plank, every joist
I've spliced into a house
for nobody but us.
You're the last of our line.
Stick fast, then; don't give
half-an-inch while you live,
not half-an-inch, d'you hear?
I've named you my heir,
I have that. Never fret,
you'll inherit the lot.
BRAND: So that's what makes you crawl
bent double. All that coin,
it's weighing you down.
MOTHER [shrinking away from him]:
Eh, what? What? Keep away!
Help! Murder! Robbery!
　　[Calmer]

Stay there. I've half a mind
to tan your hide, you brat!
I've said, you'll get it all.
Every day, bit by bit,
I crawl nearer the grave.
And then it's yours. Believe
me, everything I've earned.
You'll never need to beg.
But carry it on me?
I'm not mad! It's at home,
all snug in wad and bag.
Keep off, you varmint,
do as you're bidden,
wait till I'm gone!
As God's my judge I shan't
bury it in the midden
or under the hearth-stone
or under the floor;
shan't cram it in crevices
or such-like places.
It's yours, that I swear!

BRAND: On condition, no doubt.
You'd better spell it out!

MOTHER: Get wed; get your own brood,
lad; that's the sole task
I set you now; I ask
no other reward.
Keep my treasure safe,
eh? Guard it with your life.
Don't give nor divide.
Save everything; hide
everything you save,
like in the troll-king's cave.

BRAND [*after a short pause*]:
Ever since I was a boy
I've had to defy
you. I was never your child.

MOTHER: Agh, then be obstinate,

be sure you don't thaw!
It's little enough I care
For your love, or your hate.
I'm used to the cold,
can live without fire,
just so long as I know
that you'll breed and hoard.
Give me your word.

BRAND [*moving a step closer*]:
But what if I've a mind
to scatter it on the wind,
all that treasure of yours?

MOTHER [*reeling back in horror*]:
No, curse you! All those years
raking it together
while I grew old and my flesh
withered to ash.

BRAND: Ash on the wind, Mother.

MOTHER: You'd scatter my soul
on the wind!

BRAND: Shall
I scatter it, all the same?
Supposing I come
and stand by your bed
the first night that you're dead
and lying cold and quiet
with the psalm-book pressed
against your stone-cold heart;
suppose that I'm there,
not 'mourning the deceased',
but rummaging for treasure,
ferreting around
for what bits I can find . . .

MOTHER [*approaching, tense*]:
Where d'you get such ideas?

BRAND: You truly wish to know?

MOTHER: Yes.

BRAND: Then I'll tell you a story.

It's here in my memory,
burned deep, the scar
of an early fear.
It was one autumn;
it was one evening; a room
candle-lit, shadowy.
There my father lay.
I'd sneaked in; I stayed,
bewildered, afraid,
like a little owl,
crouched there, very still,
wondering why he slept
on and on, why he gripped
his old psalm-book,
why his hands were claw-like
and yet so paper-thin.
And then . . . and then . . .
Mother, I can still hear
those footsteps at the door;
and again the door hinge
creaks open and that strange-
faced woman creeps in.
I mustn't be seen!
Into the shadows, hide!
She goes to the bedside.
Now she begins to feel
between the bed and the wall,
pushing aside his head.
Something's there. Yes, tied;
flat oilcloth bound with twine.
It won't come undone.
She tears at it with her nails, bites
and gnaws through the tough knots,
stares, throws it down, gropes again.
A pocket-book and some coin.
She mutters between her teeth,
'How much was it all worth,
then? How much? How much?'

Like stripping the corpse, the search
proceeds. Her shadow swoops; it looks
like a swooping hawk's.
She tears open a purse
as a hawk rips a mouse.
When there's no place left
she's a woman bereft,
whispering in disbelief,
'Was that all, was that all?';
flees like a hunted thief.
So ends my tale.

MOTHER: It was what I was owed.
God knows I'd paid.

BRAND: You paid twice over, then.
It cost you your son.

MOTHER: You pay for what you get,
with brain and heart
if need be. I did,
a lot more than most.
Something was sacrificed,
something; I can't recall
what it was I had,
but it was good. I believe
people called it love.
Such things aren't practical.
But it was hard at first
to turn from my own choice,
to heed my father's voice:
'Forget that pauper-lad,
take the old man instead,
he'll feather your nest!'
So I did as he said;
and, for all that, I was cheated.
Oh but I've sweated
and I've made my pile.
With pain and with graft
I've made well-nigh double
what that old fool left.

But it's been bitter-hard.
BRAND: Hard indeed, Mother. Harder still
for your poor pawned soul.
MOTHER: I've taken care of that.
You'll get the estate,
I'll get the last rites.
I call that fair profits
for honest dealing.
My worldly goods
in exchange for priest's words
of comfort and healing.
I made you a priest.
I claim my interest.
BRAND: In the world's looking-glass
you don't see what is,
you see some other sight.
And there are many more
in these parts who stare
into that same mirror
of vanity and error.
Sparing their child a thought
now and then, they think,
'That child has me to thank
for his place in the world',
casting upon the child
the shoddy, second-hand
sentiments of their kind.
And they put all their faith
in a kind of living death.
Not knowing how to live,
they stupidly believe
eternity's the sum
of endless earthly time.
MOTHER: Can't you leave folk alone?
I'll swear you've never known
the half I've suffered!
Take what you're offered.
BRAND: That won't cancel the debt.

MOTHER: What are you on about?
    There's no debt.
BRAND: So you say.
    But supposing there were,
    would not justice require
    that each claim should be met
    in full, and by me?
MOTHER: Is that what the law says?
BRAND: Your pen-and-parchment laws!
    Mother, the Holy Spirit
    utters its own decrees,
    summons us to atone
    for what others have done.
    How blindly you have sinned!
    Open your eyes;
    begin to understand.
        [*His* MOTHER *appears confused.*]
    Don't be afraid.
    Your great debt shall be paid.
    God's image, that you've marred,
    shall shine again, purified;
    resurrected by my will;
    transfigured in my soul.
    Go to your grave in peace.
    I shall pay the price.
MOTHER: Let's see now; does that mean
    every last little sin?
BRAND: The debt. Only the debt.
    I can rid you of that.
    I am able to erase
    the effect, but not the cause.
    I cannot annul
    that sin which engendered all;
    I cannot assuage or share
    that guilt by which you *are*.
    That bears a penalty
    which you alone must pay.
MOTHER [*uneasy*]:

You're making my head spin,
just like too much sun.
Bad thoughts sprout in my head
like henbane or bindweed.
I've had enough. I'm going
back where I belong.
Under the glacier,
there I'll feel easier.

BRAND: Then go, Mother, go back;
hobble into the dark.
I'll stay here, close at hand.
If you long for me, send
for me; I shall come.

MOTHER: You'll come. Ay, to condemn!

BRAND: As your son, as your priest,
I'll shield you from the blast
of judgement and dread,
melt the ice from your blood.
I'll sing you to sleep
with psalms of sure hope.

MOTHER: You'd swear that on the Good
Book, and all?

BRAND: When I'm sent
word that you repent,
I shall come, as I said.
Like you, Mother, I make
one condition: give back
all that you have gained. Go
naked to the grave.

MOTHER: Oh no,
son, no! Tell me to starve
and thirst. Tell me I must,
I will. Don't make me give
away what I love the most.

BRAND: Everything you're worth,
or abide His wrath!

MOTHER: Everything? I can't, son, I
can't! Not every penny!

BRAND: I see you'll not atone
    till, like Job, all alone,
    covered in earth and ash,
    you cry, 'Let the day perish
    wherein this carcass came
    forth out of the womb!'

MOTHER [*wringing her hands*]:
    I can't bear it; I'm
    going, while I still can; home
    to cradle my sweet gold
    as if it was my child
    and weep for it, like
    a mother will
    for her bairn that's sick.
    Why does God leave a soul
    stuck like this in the flesh
    where your heart's dearest wish
    makes your soul die?
    Stay by me, Pastor,
    in my last hour
    and help me out.
    But until then
    let me hold on
    to the things I've got.
       [*Exit.*]

BRAND [*following her with his eyes*]:
    Yes, your pastor will stay.
    And you will send for him.
    And he shall come to warm
    your withered hand in his,
    and let you die in peace.
       [*Goes down the slope towards* AGNES]
    My life was like this sun at dawn.
    But now the sun is going down.
    At daybreak I could hear the song
    of battle; and my heart was strong.

AGNES [*turning round and looking up at him with shining eyes*]:
    The dawn was pale compared to this

full radiance. It was fantasies
and games and pretty lies and art
and everything that truth is not.
The dawn was a false paradise.
Truth must rejoice at such a loss.

BRAND: But how I dreamed! Such dreams I had,
like flocks of wild swans overhead
that swooped and bore me up, their wings
the murmur of the multitudes.
What vistas of imaginings
I saw outspread; and what clear roads
and distances to lead me on,
God's warrior of world renown!
What hymns and incense and what gold
banners brilliantly unfurled,
my triumph splendidly austere!
In spirit I was taken up
to a high place, was tempted there
with visions of exalted hope
that faded even as they shone
and turned to darkness and to stone.
Now, shadowed by these walls
of rock, where the light fades
hours before night falls,
and the fjord waters hem
me in, once more I stand
in the place I must call home.
There will be no more rides
on cloud-pawing Pegasus.
Unsaddled is that wing'd horse.
And no trumpets sound.
But let us not . . . let us not
falter, nor stoop to regret
triumphs that might have been.
I have received the sign.
I see, now, the true goal
to strive for: humble toil
ennobled by belief,

the sacrificial life.

AGNES: But what of that false god
who was to be destroyed,
you said? Will he not fall,
then? Ever?

BRAND: Fall he shall!
But not in the wild gaze
of crowds, not to their vast applause.
I was wrong, I was wrong.
In vain we stir the soil
round the roots of the soul
unless that soul is strong.
It is not raucous fame
that redeems the time.
It is the will alone
that can purge and refine,
that alone has the power
to make or mar
what we do, whether the work
be famed or not.

> [*He turns towards the village, where the evening shadows are beginning to gather.*]
                    You who walk
with slow and sullen step
in the narrow and steep
places of this land,
I shall teach you to praise,
with heart and mind and hand
in true communion
one with another; to rouse
from mortal sleep the young lion
of the immortal will.
Let us do all things well,
let the pickaxe, the spade,
shine like the battle blade.
Then shall the hand of God
inscribe His holy word
upon the human heart

as though on Sinai slate.
Let nobleness appear,
let those who faint and fear
find strength. Righteousness shall destroy
falsehood utterly.

[*He begins to leave.* EINAR *meets him.*]

EINAR: You there! Yes, you, sir! Give me back
that which you took!

BRAND: That which . . . ? Ah! Speak to her.
Speak, but will she hear?

EINAR: Agnes, I beg you, stay;
stay on the sunlit heights,
not where dark sorrow sits.

AGNES: I have no choice to make.
I have one road to take.
This is the only way.

EINAR: How can you? How can you leave
your mother, your sisters?

AGNES: Give
them my love. I shall send
a letter when I have found
words to express
what my soul clearly sees.

EINAR: Out there, where the great waters gleam,
the white-sailed vessels scud and skim,
dipping their prows in pearly foam,
bright emanations of a dream,
seeking the fabled shore, the calm
landfall and their longed-for home.

AGNES: Sail with them, then, go east or
west; but think of me as dead.

EINAR: Come, come with me; my sister
if not my bride!

AGNES: Einar, Einar, I have told
you. There is an ocean
of silence. It lies between
us, wider than the world.

EINAR: Go home, then. Go, be safe!

AGNES [*softly*]:
    This man is my whole life.
BRAND: Young woman, beware.
    And when you choose, be sure.
    For, choosing, you are chosen
    In the shadow of these frozen
    peaks, I shall remain
    a forgotten man.
    And life with me will seem
    an endless winter gloom.
AGNES: Starshine pierces the cloud.
    I am not afraid.
BRAND: All or nothing. That
    is my demand. The task
    is very great. And the risk,
    also, is very great.
    There'll be no mercy shown.
    There's no provision made
    for weakness or dread.
    Falter, and you go down
    into the depths of the sea.
    Mere lifelong sacrifice
    itself may not suffice.
    Would you die willingly?
EINAR: This is no seaside game.
    It is a dark and cruel
    commandment that can kill.
BRAND [*to* AGNES]:
    You stand where the roads cross.
    Once and for all, then! Choose!
        [*Exit.*]
EINAR: Choose between storm and calm.
    Choose between 'go' and 'stay'.
    Choose between joy and grief.
    Choose between night and day.
    Choose between death and life.
AGNES: Beyond darkness and death
    light dawns upon the earth.

[*She follows* BRAND. EINAR *looks for some time, as if lost, in the direction in which she has gone; then he bows his head and goes out towards the fjord again.*]

ACT THREE

Three years later. A small garden at the Pastor's house. A high mountain face above it, a stone wall around it. The fjord, narrow and shut in, in the background. The door of the house leads into the garden. Afternoon. BRAND *stands on the steps outside the house.* AGNES *sits on the step below him.*

AGNES: My dear, why do you gaze
    endlessly over the fjord,
    and with such anxious eyes,
    unwilling to rest?
BRAND: These three years past
    I've waited for some word
    from my mother. Now I hear
    she lies at death's door;
    yet I've received no sign
    that she's dead to her sin.
    Therefore I wait.
AGNES [*softly and lovingly*]:
    Why do you hesitate
    to go now? Go to her,
    go to her!
BRAND [*shaking his head*]:
             Let her repent,
    then; let her sacrifice
    everything that she has.
    No solace, no sacrament,
    until that's done.
AGNES: But your
    own mother, Brand . . .
BRAND: Own? Own?

Would you have me bow down
to every household god
of clay and blood?

AGNES: So harsh . . .

BRAND: To you?

AGNES: Ah, no.

BRAND: I saw
what must be; foresaw and foretold
struggle and bitter cold.

AGNES [*smiling*]:
O my dearest, Brand's law
sometimes is fallible,
it seems. Look, I can smile.

BRAND: Life withers; and your cheeks
grow pale now; mind and soul
burn in the icy chill.
The glacier looms; the black rocks
threaten our house.

AGNES: Look how they shelter us.
Hidden under the glacier's rim
we're safe; and when, in spring, the stream
leaps from the cliff, we live
snug and unharmed
behind the waterfall
in our ferny cave.

BRAND: In a deep cave, unwarmed
by any shred of sun.

AGNES: Isn't the sun-
light lovely to look at when
it shines on the high fell!

BRAND: Shines, Agnes? When? For a few weeks
perhaps, a brief glimmer
at midsummer.

AGNES [*looking firmly at him and getting up*]:
There's something here that makes
even you afraid.

BRAND: Surely it is *your* heart
that's thrilled by some secret

dread, some abyss of dread.
It's as though you stand
staring into that abyss.

AGNES: Sometimes, I confess,
sometimes, yes, I've trembled . . .

BRAND: Trembled?

AGNES: For our child,
for Alf.

BRAND: For Alf!

AGNES: Ah, you see, Brand,
you tremble too!

BRAND: Agnes, at times
I fear for our little son.
But he'll get well;
God is just; not cruel . . .
not cruel . . . Where is Alf now?

AGNES: Asleep.

BRAND [*looking in through the door*]:
                    So he is! No dreams
of sickness or pain
haunt his pillow
with their gaunt phantom shapes.

AGNES: But he's so pale.

BRAND: It will pass,
it will pass.

AGNES: How sweetly he sleeps.

BRAND [*closing the door*]:
Sleep and grow strong. God bless
you, my own child! God bless you both
for the gifts that you bring with
such an instinct of grace. Labour
and grief, now, are easy to bear.
Day after day I am filled
with new strength as the child
plays, as I watch him at play.
God summoned me to stay.
I made the sacrifice.
It seemed a martyrdom

that I embraced. How altered
now: here, in the wilderness,
manna for one who starved.

AGNES: For one who toiled, and served,
and never faltered.
I know what tears you've shed
in secret, tears of blood.
You have earned your fame.

BRAND: Love touched me; now each thing
I do is blest. Spring awakening
in heart and in mind,
that is what I have found
with you, and with none other.
Neither father nor mother
had kindled the least spark
of love. I do believe all
the tenderness of my soul
that was clamped into the dark
is here released to shine
on what is truly mine.

AGNES: And upon all who come
to your hearth and home:
the poor and the downtrodden,
the fatherless child, bidden
to enter, each one a guest
at your heart's truth's feast.

BRAND: What I am, what I do, I owe
to Alf and to you: two
souls who crossed the gulf
into my inmost self.
I was too long alone.
Spirit had become stone.

AGNES: Where you caress, you strike.
Those whom you bless, you break.

BRAND: Not you, Agnes?

AGNES: No, Brand.
But that which you demand,
'all or nothing', has driven

souls out of Heaven.

BRAND: That which the world calls 'love'
    I do not wish to have.
    God's love is hard to bear,
    I know that. Those who fear
    have cause enough to dread
    the summons. When Christ prayed,
    'Lord, take away this cup',
    shivering in his sweat,
    what answer did he get?
    None. Christ had to drain
    the terror and the pain
    and taste the dregs.

AGNES: What hope
    is there for us poor souls
    weighed on such judgement scales?

BRAND: Who's doomed by God's just law?
    Oh do not seek to know!
    Enough that you understand
    'Be faithful and endure'
    written by His own hand
    in letters of fire.
    To those who, striving, fall,
    God will be merciful.
    Those who refuse to strive
    He will not forgive.
    Agnes, in my book
    the first commandment says,
    'You shall not compromise'.
    Half-done, ill-done work
    thwarting the soul's power,
    dooms the ill-doer.
    Yes, Agnes, it is so.

AGNES [*throwing her arms around his neck*]:
    Where you go, I shall go.

BRAND: Where love goes, no road
    is too steep or hard.

        [*The DOCTOR has come down the road and stops out-*

side the garden wall.]

DOCTOR: And what are you doing?
Ah, billing and cooing
among these sylvan groves,
pretty turtle-doves!

AGNES [*running to open the garden gate*]:
Doctor, come in! Do, please!

DOCTOR: Now you know very well
that I won't. I'm so cross.
Really, why must you stay
in this place? Call it 'home'?
It's a troll-cave of gloom,
all glacier, no sky.
Brr . . . it shrivels your soul!

BRAND: Not my soul.

DOCTOR: Tch, man!
You know what I mean.
With you, 'a promise made
is a promise kept' indeed.

AGNES: Where love is, there's no need of sun
to bring the whole of summer in.

DOCTOR: H'm. I've a call to make.

BRAND: My mother?

DOCTOR: Very sick.
A few more hours, and then . . .
But you know that of course.
You'll have been to her house.
Just back, are you?

BRAND: I've not been.

DOCTOR: Well, now I've heard it all!
I've trudged mile after mile
across whinstone and bog,
tight-fisted old hag
though she is, just for her!

BRAND: God bless you for that —
all your skill and care.

DOCTOR: God bless my soft heart.
Perhaps you'd rather

that we went there together . . .

BRAND: Doctor, unless I hear
    that she's ready to pay
    the full penalty,
    not one inch will I stir.

DOCTOR [*to* AGNES]:
    His heart's as hard as rock.
    You poor defenceless lamb,
    I'm sorry for your sake.

AGNES: Don't be. What's more, he'd give
    all his heart's blood to save
    that woman's soul.

BRAND: I am her son.
    Am I not pledged to atone,
    to honour every claim?
    I tell you, every debt
    shall be wiped out!

DOCTOR: By one who's a pauper
    himself? Most improper.

BRAND: I have made my choice
    freely. Let that suffice.

DOCTOR [*looking hard at him*]:
    Pastor, your ledger's full
    of 'God's law' and 'man's will'.
    But the column marked 'love',
    that's still blank, I believe.
        [*Exit.*]

BRAND [*gazing after him for a while*]:
    Nothing is so much soiled
    by the commerce of the world
    as the word 'love': this veil
    hiding the deformed soul.
    Man's pathway's dark and steep:
    here's 'love' to guide his step.
    He wallows in his sin:
    'love' hauls him out again.
    He cringes from the fight:
    with 'love' there's no defeat.

AGNES: I know such things are false.
    Love is something else.
BRAND: Agnes, if souls are athirst
    for truth and righteousness,
    let us assuage that longing first;
    then speak of love.
    Merely to perish on the cross,
    or to writhe in the flame,
    daily to be buried alive,
    this is not martyrdom.
    But to make a burnt offering
    out of the suffering,
    to ordain the anguish
    of our spirit and our flesh,
    that is salvation, there we seize
    hold of martyrdom's prize!
AGNES [*clinging tightly to him*]:
    Brand, when I weaken,
    when I flinch from the task,
    speak then as you have spoken
    now. That much I do ask.
BRAND: Man's will must blaze the way
    for God's victory,
    so that love can alight,
    the white dove with the olive-leaf
    of mercy and new life.
    But – until then – hate!
      [*In terror*]
    Hatred, the one redeeming word!
    Hatred, the angel of the Lord!
      [*He hurries into the house.*]
AGNES [*looking in through the open door*]:
    Now he's with Alf, kneeling by his bed.
    I think he's crying; he rocks
    to and fro, to and fro. He seeks
    comfort; that great-hearted man
    seeks comfort from a child
    innocent of the world.

But he's . . . is the child ill? What is it?
    [*Cries out in fear*]
Brand, what is it? What have you seen
that makes you so afraid?
    [BRAND *comes out on to the steps.*]
BRAND: Was that . . . ? I heard the gate,
  I thought. No messenger?
AGNES: None.
BRAND [*looking back into the house*]:
          His pulse is much too fast
  and his skin's like fire.
  Agnes, be strong.
AGNES: I tremble
  when you say that.
BRAND: Be strong.
    [*Looking along the road*]
               At last!
A MESSENGER [*coming through the garden gate*]:
  She'll not live long . . .
BRAND: What message do you bring?
MESSENGER: A right old jumble.
  She sat up and screeched,
  'I want the priest fetched;
  my son, mind! Tell him, "half." '
BRAND [*shrinking back*]: Half? No!
MESSENGER: Half, I swear,
  as true as I stand here.
BRAND: You misheard. She said, 'all'.
MESSENGER: Look, man, I'm not deaf.
  I know what I heard.
  'Half' is what she said.
BRAND: You'd swear that, at the Day
  of Judgement?
    [*He clutches the* MESSENGER'*s arm.*]
MESSENGER: On my soul.
BRAND [*firmly*]:
  Then take her my reply:
  'No bread, no wine,

no comfort, none.'

MESSENGER [*looking uncertainly at him*]:
    Perhaps *your* hearing's bad.
    She's dying, your own mother . . .
BRAND: I don't make different laws,
    one for my own hearth, the other
    for strangers. My mother knows
    that 'all or nothing'
    is absolute. One piece
    struck from the Golden Calf
    is an idol, no less
    than the beast itself.
MESSENGER: Well, if she's still breathing
    by the time I get back,
    I'll tell her, 'Your son
    sends his best wishes –
    fifty lashes!'
    I shan't relish the work,
    I tell you plain.
    How can you treat her so?
    God himself is less hard.
    That's a comfort anyhow!
       [*Exit.*]
BRAND: This stinking comfort blown
    from their own carrion;
    the stench of deathly fear
    tainting the world's air!
    Even their so-called faith
    they keep to bargain with,
    to bribe their senile judge,
    a sop to soothe his rage.
       [*Out in the road, the* MESSENGER *has met a*
       SECOND MESSENGER; *both return.*]
    Another message?
FIRST MESSENGER: Yes.
BRAND: What does she say?
SECOND MESSENGER: She says,
    'Nine-tenths.'

BRAND: She's not said 'all'?

SECOND MESSENGER: She's not.

BRAND: Go back, then; tell
her, 'No wine, no bread,
no comfort.'

SECOND MESSENGER: Hasn't she paid
enough? More than enough?

FIRST MESSENGER: That woman gave you life.

BRAND [*clenching his hands*]:
What would you have me do?
Deal kindly with what's mine
and deal harshly with you?

SECOND MESSENGER: Her need, her dread, are terrible
to see. Give her some sign.

BRAND [*to the* FIRST MESSENGER]:
No sacraments can be brought
to an unclean table:
tell her what I have said.
      [*The* MESSENGERS *leave.*]

AGNES [*clinging to him*]:
Brand, sometimes you seem
like some grim scourge of God,
like God's own sword of flame.
I flinch from the sight.

BRAND [*sorrowfully*]:
But, Agnes, the world's sword
has already drawn blood
from me; many times it has cut
me to the heart.

AGNES: Your own demands go deep;
they're not easy to bear.
How many measure up
to such morality?
Pitifully few, I fear.

BRAND: This entire age is devoid
of grace or merit;
it's ruled by creeping pride,
dull frivolity,

meanness of spirit.
Say to the 'man-of-the-hour',
whether of peace or war,
'Enough; be satisfied
with the true victory,
with the triumph of good;
let your own name go down
to dust; let silence reign.'
Would he agree?
Or tell some eager poet
with his sweet cage-birds of song,
tell *him* to live unsung.
He'd fly at your throat.
Rich men who set such store
by largesse to the poor
bargain on gratitude
posthumously accrued.
But selfless charity,
now there's a rarity!
The mighty and the meek,
the strong man and the sick,
are all alike in this
loathing of sacrifice,
this craving to possess,
this thraldom to the world.
In dread of the abyss
they struggle to keep hold,
clinging to root and branch
until the avalanche.

AGNES: Yet still you thunder 'all
or nothing' as they fall.

BRAND: Lose all if you would gain
all. Out of the depths men
scale even the precipice
of their own fall from grace.
    [*Silent for a moment*]
Everything that I speak
is spoken in agony.

I'm like a castaway
crying in vain among
the spars of a great wreck.
I could bite out my tongue
that must rage and chastise
and with its prophecies
strike terror where I crave
the touch of human love.
Watch over our child,
Agnes. In a radiant dream
his spirit lies so calm,
like water that is stilled,
like a mountain tarn
silent under the sun.
Sometimes his mother's face
hovers over that hushed place,
is received, is given back,
as beautifully as a bird
hovers, and hovering, is mirror'd
in the depths of the lake.

AGNES [*pale*]:
No matter where you aim
your thoughts, they fly to him.

BRAND: O Agnes, guard him well,
in quietness.

AGNES: I will.
Only . . . a few more
words . . .

BRAND: Words to inspire!

AGNES: All the strength you can give.

BRAND [*embracing her*]:
The innocent shall live.

AGNES [*looking up radiantly*]:
The innocent! You see, even
God dare not destroy
such a gift from Heaven!
          [*She goes into the house.*]

BRAND [*gazing silently; then*]:

Does she think God has qualms? –
the God who chose Abraham's
belovèd child, the boy
Isaac, as the altar stone
of his father's faith!
　　　[*Shakes off his thoughts*]
No! I've made my sacrifice.
The great cause is forgone,
and I've stifled the voice
that could rouse the whole earth
to His redeeming wrath:
'You sleepers, wake!' I've come
down from that high dream.
　　　[*Looks down the road*]
This torment of delay!
Why no repentance, why?
Why is she not prepared,
even in this last pain,
to be rid of her sin,
to tear its claggy root
out of her heart?
　　　[*The* MAYOR *appears on the road, walking in the
　　　direction of the Pastor's house.*]
A message! Yes, the word
at last! Ugh, no. The Mayor,
look at him, tasting the air,
strutting and jolly,
his hands in his pockets,
his arms like brackets
around his belly.
MAYOR [*through the garden gate*]:
Good day, Reverend!
How are you, friend?
I fear I've come
at a difficult time.
Your mother, I believe,
not much longer to live?
Very distressing!

Death comes to us all.
As I was passing
I thought, 'Why not call?
Very much better
to tackle the matter
head-on.' It's well known
you're at daggers drawn.
BRAND: At daggers drawn?
MAYOR: That's what they say.
Her treasure's under lock and key.
BRAND: The reckoning's overdue;
    that at least is true.
MAYOR: As soon as the old girl
    (God rest her soul)
    lies in Mother Earth,
    just think what you'll be worth!
    The world's your oyster
    from now on, Pastor.
    Believe me, I know.
BRAND: That means 'Be off with you!'
MAYOR: Best thing for all concerned.
    I'm sure you understand.
    We're happy as we are,
    we liege-folk of the shore.
    Your spiritual fire,
    utterly wasted here!
BRAND: A man's own native soil
    sustains him; he best thrives
    where he first plants his foot.
    If he's cast out, his soul
    withers; nothing he strives
    for blossoms or bears fruit.
MAYOR: A man must do what's best
    in the national interest.
BRAND: How can you ever truly
    know what our country needs,
    if you bury your heads
    deep in this darkling valley?

Go, purify your sight
in the clear air of the height!
MAYOR: That sounds like city talk,
Pastor. We're humble folk.
BRAND: These boundaries you draw
between 'high' and 'low'!
This never-ending wail,
'We are small, we are small, we are small!'
MAYOR: For everything there is a time
and a due season, says the psalm.
This lowly parish, sir, has cast
its mite into the treasure-chest
of weighty cause and doughty deed,
a credit to our Viking blood!
Those sagas, those heroic lays
of good King Bele's golden days
and those great brothers, Ulf and Thor,
and many a hundred heroes more!
Some say it's not polite to boast,
some say, 'Forget what's dead and past';
but I, for one, am very proud
of what our great forefathers did.
Few have done better, I'll be bound,
to aid the progress of mankind!
BRAND: But you even betray
your own battle-cry,
your 'patriots' pledge',
your *'noblesse oblige'*!
What do you care
for that 'goodly fere',
King Bele's men?
You've ploughed them in!
MAYOR: But you're wrong, you're wrong!
Why don't you come along
to our next 'wassail'
in the parish hall?
The schoolmaster, magistrate,
myself, all the élite

of the neighbourhood,
pounding the festal board
and drinking hot toddy!
King Bele lives, laddy!
At such times I feel stirred
by the power of the word,
by heroic verse.
I'm partial to a bit
of rhyming; and that goes,
I'd say, for most of us
round here. Enough's enough,
though. Art isn't life,
as I hope you'll agree. But,
say, between seven and ten
of an evening, when work's
over and folk can relax,
we dally with the muse,
and pipe a lyric strain,
we play at hunt-the-rhyme,
and bathe in the sublime.
Now, just between ourselves,
Pastor, there's something odd
in your whole attitude.
You don't do things by halves.
We do. You want to fight,
turn every wrong to right
at one fell swoop, it seems.
These, I think, are your aims?
Correct me, if they're not.
BRAND: Something of the sort.
MAYOR: Keep your lofty ideals
for your intellectuals
in the big city.
We're tillers of the soil,
we're toilers of the sea.
BRAND: Then justify that toil!
Into the ocean cast
each vainglorious boast;

and deep in the earth hide
every platitude.
MAYOR: Surely great nations thrive
on memories!
BRAND: If you have
nothing but memories
you keep vigil in vain
at an empty cairn.
MAYOR: It's plain you're much too good
for this neighbourhood.
Look, leave it to me –
I'll soon restore morale
among our 'sons of toil'.
That I can guarantee.
It's not too much to claim
that my mayoral term
has won deserved applause
for grit and enterprise.
Why, the birth-rate has increased
thanks to my zeal and zest!
What wonders men perform,
under their own steam!
A new road or a bridge,
real marvels of the age!
BRAND: Between the life of earth
and the living faith
you've built nothing at all.
MAYOR: My new road to the fell!
BRAND: Between vision and deed
I see no new road;
but I have seen God's hand
writing His words of flame:
'The place where you are come
is your abiding place.'
Here I take my stand.
MAYOR: Well, stay if you must.
But stick to your last;
castigate crime and vice,

God knows, there's need enough,
wickedness is rife.
But we don't want fuss.
And please remember this:
six whole days a week
are devoted to work.
One day for sober thought
is more than adequate.
And don't expect the Lord
God to walk on the fjord,
either!

BRAND: To make use
of such practical advice
I would have to change
souls, or my soul's range
of vision. Souls are called
by God, not by the world.
And I shall set free
by my soul's victory
the people whom you led,
lulled and betrayed,
starved and constrained
with your poverty of mind.

MAYOR: So we're to fight it out?
You'll be the first to fall.
Mark my words, you will!

BRAND: Victorious in defeat.
You'll never understand . . .

MAYOR: And can you wonder? Friend,
don't turn your back on life!
Don't hazard every good
that this world has bestowed
with such generous hands –
your mother's gold, her bonds,
your child and your good wife.

BRAND: And if I must renounce
such an inheritance?
And if I must, what then?

73

MAYOR: It doesn't make sense!
    You haven't a chance!
    Think on, think on!
BRAND: Here's where I stake my claim;
    here, in my own home;
    and if I shrink from the call
    I lose my own soul.
MAYOR: But a man on his own
    can't hope to win.
BRAND: The best are on my side.
MAYOR [*smiling*]:
    I've thousands on parade!
        [*Exit.*]
BRAND [*gazing after him*]:
    There goes a stalwart democrat,
    filled with the democratic urge,
    the proper sentiments at heart;
    but what a scourge!
    No avalanche or hurricane
    has done the damage he has done
    with a good conscience all these years.
    How many smiles he's turned to tears!
    What gifts, what ardours, have recoiled
    to darkness, all their music stilled.
    What impulses of joy or wrath
    he cheerfully deprives of breath.
    How many hearts has he destroyed,
    without the slightest trace of blood!
        [*The* DOCTOR *appears at the garden gate.* BRAND
        suddenly notices him and cries out in anguish]
    Doctor! Is there some word?
        [*He runs to meet him.*]
DOCTOR: We must leave her to God . . .
    I'm sorry, my boy . . .
BRAND: But surely, before she died,
    surely she must have said . . .
DOCTOR: 'I repent, I repent!'
    Is that what you want?

She gave nothing away.

BRAND [*gazing in silence before he speaks*]:
  Then she's lost for ever?

DOCTOR: God may be less severe.
  She whispered, at the end,
  'He is kinder than Brand.'

BRAND [*sinking down, as if in pain, on the bench*]:
  In the final agony
  of guilt, on the brink of death
  itself, the same old lie.
      [*He hides his face in his hands.*]

DOCTOR [*coming nearer, looking at him and shaking his head*]:
  You live by the old law,
  do you not? Here and now,
  'An eye for an eye, a tooth
  for a tooth'. But I believe
  that each generation
  has its own life to live
  in its own fashion.
  Ours has the wit to laugh
  at every 'old wife'
  with her rag-bag of ghouls,
  changelings, damned souls,
  and dead bodies that rise.
  Our first commandment is:
  'Be humane, be humane!'

BRAND: Words foolish and vain!
  Try to make 'all or nothing'
  fit your 'humane' clothing.
  Was God 'humane' to Jesus Christ?
  Was He a bloodless altruist?
  Your God of liberal discernment
  would doubtless manage the atonement
  with a brisk noncommittal note
  like any cautious diplomat.
      [*He hides his head and sits in mute grief.*]

DOCTOR [*softly*]:
  Rage, rage, you soul in a storm,

till you have spent your force.
Better if you could weep . . .

> [AGNES *has come out on to the steps; she is pale and*
> *terrified and whispers to the* DOCTOR.]

AGNES: Doctor, please; please come;
come to the child!

DOCTOR: Of course,
my dear, of course! And stop
trembling: you'll make *me* afraid!

AGNES [*pulling him along with her*]:
Hurry, please! Merciful God!

> [*They go into the house.* BRAND *does not notice them.*]

BRAND: She died as she had lived,
past hope of being saved.
Therefore God's writ thrusts home
the justice of the claim:
her son must bear the cost
or be himself accurst.
So be it. I am sworn
from this moment on
never to turn aside
from my great crusade,
this travail towards the will's harsh
triumph over the flesh.
God is my strength. The word
of His mouth is like a sword
for me to wield. His wrath
kindles my very breath.
I am possessed of His will.
I shall make mountains fall.

> [*The* DOCTOR, *followed by* AGNES, *comes hurriedly*
> *out on to the steps.*]

DOCTOR: Get ready at once, and leave.

BRAND: If I felt the whole earth
shudder, I would not move.

DOCTOR: Then your child will die;
you have condemned him to death.

BRAND [*bewildered; making to go into the house*]:

Alf? What troll-tale is this?
DOCTOR [*holding him back*]: Stay
a moment. Tell me, when
did you last see the sun?
Must I tell you how fierce
the gusts are; how the fog
is like the breath of the ice?
Your house is an iceberg.
One more winter spent
here, and your tender plant
will perish. Go! Go soon!
Tomorrow if you can.
BRAND: This very evening.
Agnes, we'll lift him up
gently in his sleep.
No more shall the ravening
ice-winds from the shore
scorch him with their cold fire.
Never again shall he feel
the glacier's deathly chill.
We must find a new home
far away where it's warm,
where he can thrive and grow.
Hurry! Hurry now!
Death is a web that's spun
Stronger each minute!
AGNES: I've known
a secret dread. In my heart
I foresaw this threat;
I feared for his life.
But not enough.
BRAND [*to the* DOCTOR]:
If we make our escape
now, there truly is hope
that his health will improve?
I have your word?
DOCTOR: You have.
BRAND: Doctor, you've saved my son.

77

Agnes, be sure to fold
round him the warm eider-down.
The evening air strikes cold.

> [AGNES *goes into the house. The* DOCTOR *gazes silently at* BRAND *who stands motionless looking in through the door; then he goes up to him, putting his hand on his shoulder.*]

DOCTOR: For a man without remorse
you're quick to compromise
when the lamb to be slain
is yours, your own first-born.
One law for the world,
another for your child,
a double standard,
is that it? You thundered
'all or nothing' in the ears
of those poor villagers
in their terror and want.
You refused to forgive
your mother unless she went
naked to the grave.
But now it's your turn
to be the shipwrecked man
clinging to the keel
in the howling gale.
What good are they now,
those tables of the law?
Your sermons on hell-fire,
what a burden they are!
Jettison them!
Now it's sink or swim;
and it's 'God keep him safe,
my own darling boy!'
You'd best be on your way.
Take your child and your wife
and go. And don't glance back
at your forsaken flock.
And don't spare a thought

for the hapless plight
of your mother's soul.
Renounce the call.
Farewell, then, Priest!
'*Consummatum est!*'

[BRAND *clutches his head in bewilderment as if to col-
lect his thoughts.*]

BRAND: Have I been struck blind?
Or was I blind before?
DOCTOR: Please don't misunderstand.
I entirely applaud
this change in your mood.
I very much prefer
the new family man
to the old man–of–iron.
Believe me, I've spoken out
for your own good. I've put
a mirror in your hand.
Look hard at what you find.

[*Exit.*]

BRAND [*gazing for a while in front of him; then suddenly
exclaiming*]:
As I am now . . . as I was then . . .
where does truth end, error begin . . . ?
Blind man or seer, which man am I?

[AGNES *comes out of the house with a cloak over her
shoulders and the child in her arms.* BRAND *does not
see her. She makes as if to speak, but stops as if struck by
terror when she sees the expression on his face. At the
same moment a* MAN *comes hurriedly through the
garden gate. The sun sets.*]

MAN: A word in your ear.
Watch out for the Mayor.
You've roused an enemy.
BRAND [*pressing his hand against his breast*]:
An enemy indeed!
MAN: He's after your blood.
The good seed you'd sown,

thriving it was;
ay, really thriving.
Then up he slinks and says,
'The Pastor's leaving.
I told you he would;
I said he'd be gone
at the first chink of gold.'
Well, that was that:
Mildew and blight!

BRAND: If what he said was true . . . ?

MAN: Nay, Pastor, not you!
We all know the reason
he's spreading poison.
You always speak your mind;
and you won't break nor bend.
That's what he can't abide.

BRAND: But suppose he's not lied . . .

MAN: Then you've betrayed us all;
and yourself as well.
Again and again you've said
how you've been summoned by God,
how your heart's home is here,
how you're fighting this war
right through to the end,
here on your home ground;
how brave men, once they're called,
can't quit the fight, nor yield.
It's been like a great song
you've sung us. Ay, and strong
and steady is the flame
you've lit in many hearts.

BRAND: A rabble of deaf-mutes,
and sleepers who won't wake.
This battle's not for them.

MAN: Pastor, it is; as you
well know! Things gleam and glow
as never before, like the sunrise in Heaven!

BRAND: One in ten
    thousand turns to the light.
    The rest crouch in the dark.
MAN: You are a torch in the night!
    I'm not booklearned, sir.
    I live by inward prayer.
    It's you that's lugged me out
    from the depths of the pit.
    If you let go, I'm lost.
    You can't! I hold you fast!
    Bless you, sir! Praise the Lord!
    You'll not play false to Him;
    nor leave us to our doom.
        [*Exit.*]
AGNES [*timidly*]:
    Your cheeks are deathly white;
    your lips are bloodless; it
    seems that your very heart
    is crying out, 'I'm hurt.'
BRAND: Every resounding word
    is my accuser now.
    My own prophetic voice
    echoes with mocking force
    from that blank face of snow.
AGNES [*taking a step forward*]:
    I am prepared.
BRAND: Prepared? Prepared for what?
AGNES [*forcefully*]:
    For all that I must meet.
        [GERD *runs past on the road outside and stops at the*
        garden gate.]
GERD [*clapping her hands and shouting with a wild joy*]:
    Hey! Have you heard?
    The priest's flown away.
    And now the throngs
    of dwarfs and trolls,
    all swart and spry,
    swarm on the hills.

The spiteful things,
they scratched my eyes,
look! with their claws.
And half my soul
they tweaked and stole;
left me with half
a soul for life.

BRAND: Curb your tongue, girl.
Don't prance and shrill
so! I've not gone,
you simpleton,
I'm here!

GERD: O sir,
I can see *you* are.
But you're not him.
You're not the priest,
you're not. My hawk,
it swooped and hissed,
an angry gleam
through mist and murk.
With that one swoop
it snatched him up.
Away he rode,
the priest, astride,
as though with saddle,
whip, spur, and bridle!
His church stands cold and bare,
and its poor day is done.
But mine, now! Look at mine!
It soars so close to Heaven!
A true priest worships there.
His cope is woven
from strands of ice and fire.
And when he chants and sings,
the whole earth rings.

BRAND: You witch, why do you try
to lead my soul astray
with your wild riddles

of heathen idols?

> [GERD *comes inside the garden gate.*]

GERD: Idol? What does that mean?
　　Ah . . . I know what it is.
　　Sometimes it's like a man,
　　but a giant in size.
　　Sometimes it's very small,
　　like a little doll.
　　Always it's of gold.
　　Sometimes it's like a child,
　　a child fast asleep.

> [*Points*]

　　Is that your idol? Hey,
　　don't snatch it away;
　　let me take a peep!
　　Let me touch, let me feel
　　under that pretty shawl.

AGNES [*to* BRAND]:
　　Have you any tears
　　left? Have you any prayers?
　　My sorrow's all been burnt
　　away, by dread . . .

BRAND: 　　　　　　O Agnes, this poor
　　mad creature – she has been sent
　　by some all-seeing power . . .

GERD: Listen! Listen! That sound
　　echoing round the fells!
　　Look! Look! Look how they march
　　and jostle to my church,
　　trolls that the priest had drowned,
　　all risen from the reefs,
　　all summoned by the bells!
　　Look there! A thousand dwarfs.
　　The old priest locked them in,
　　buried them in the screes,
　　sealed with his holy sign,
　　sealed with the Christians' cross.
　　Look how they rise and swarm,

troll–children, the undead,
thronging the mountainside.
How they chatter and scream,
how they whimper and cry,
'Mother! Mother!' The womenfolk
gaze on them with joy
and fondle them; and some
give them their breasts to suck.
O look, they're in a dream!
All those good pious souls
walking with the trolls
as though among their own
dear children!

BRAND: Now be gone,
will you! Out of my sight!

GERD: Look! Do you see him sit,
do you, there where the road
starts to climb to the fell?
He's writing in his book
the names of his great flock.
Soon he will have them all.
How he's laughing! He's glad
the little church stands bare,
shut with bolt and bar;
glad the old priest has flown
far away through the murk
on the great hawk's back.
Hey! Catch me if you can!

> [*She springs over the garden wall and disappears among
> the rocks. Silence.*]

AGNES [*approaching, and speaking very quietly*]:
It's time for us to go.

BRAND [*staring at her*]:
Go where, though?

> [*Points first to the garden gate, then to the door of the
> house*]

                    Out . . . or in?

AGNES [*shrinking back in terror*]:

Brand! What do you mean?
Your child . . .
BRAND [*following her*]:
                          Answer me!
    What am I first?
    His father, or their priest?
AGNES [*shrinking back even further*]:
    If a voice through a cloud
    spoke in thunder, 'Reply!',
    what could I find to say?
    Not a word, not a word.
BRAND: You have a mother's right
    to choose. This way, or that?
AGNES: Ask what you dare to ask,
    I am your wife. My task
    is simply to obey.
BRAND [*as if about to seize her arm*]:
    Then I implore you: take
    this cup of agony.
    Drink of it, for my sake.
AGNES [*drawing back*]:
    But if I did, I would not
    have a mother's heart.
BRAND: So the judgement is given . . .
AGNES: What choice do you have . . . ?
BRAND: Is given and upheld.
AGNES: Do you truly believe
    that you are called?
BRAND [*grasping her hand tightly*]:
    Yes. Is it life, or death?
AGNES: Follow your true path.
BRAND: Then let us go.
AGNES [*tonelessly*]:
                          The road,
    Brand; where does it lead?
            [BRAND *is silent.* AGNES *points to the garden gate.*]
    Is this the way?
BRAND [*pointing to the door of the house*]:

No, this.

AGNES [*lifting the child high in her arms*]:
That which you have dared
to ask of me, O Lord,
I dare to give to Heaven.
Accept my sacrifice.
Now lead me through your night.

    [*She goes into the house.* BRAND *stares blindly for a*
    moment; bursts into tears; clasps his hands over his head
    and throws himself down on the steps.]

BRAND [*crying out*]:
Lord, grant me light!

ACT FOUR

Christmas Eve in the Pastor's house. It is dark in the room. On the back wall, a door leading out; a window on one side of the stage, a door on the other. AGNES *stands dressed in mourning at the window and stares out into the darkness.*

> AGNES: Another night. And still he's not
> returned. I've waited, my heart
> heavy with cry upon cry.
> And heavily, silently,
> the snow falls. Thick and soft,
> already it has roofed
> and robed the old church in white.
> Ah, what was that? The gate!
> Footsteps, now, at the door!
> Hurry, oh hurry!
> > [*Goes to the door and opens it.* BRAND *enters, covered with snow, in travelling clothes which he throws off during the following lines.*]
> > > My dear,
> dear love, how long you've been!
> O Brand, don't ever leave me again!
> I'm lonely; I can't endure
> this shadow-house when you're
> not with me. I'm so cold.
> Comfort me!
> > [BRAND *lights a candle; it glimmers faintly in the room.*]
> BRAND: My poor child,
> how pale you look, so very pale
> in the candlelight. Are you ill?

AGNES: No, no, not ill; but tired
and faint with watching. I feared
so much for you. Look, I've twined
the few evergreens I could find
as garlands for our tree. They seem
more like wreaths, though, for him . . .
for our son . . .
   [*She begins to cry.*]
BRAND: He's dead and buried,
Agnes. So let your tears be dried.
AGNES: Be patient with me. The hurt
I had was deep. It will smart
for a while. But pain
withers. I shall be quiet soon.
BRAND: Agnes! Agnes! Is this how
you keep Christmas – with sorrow?
AGNES: I beg you: bear with my grief.
My little son . . . he was all life,
and now . . . now . . .
BRAND: In his grave.
AGNES: Don't taunt me, for the love
of God!
BRAND: It must be said.
The more you are afraid,
the more you must hear
his knell, as waves toll on the shore.
AGNES: You suffer. Will you not admit
you suffer? Even now, the sweat
glistens on your forehead.
BRAND: It's only spray from the fjord.
AGNES: That moisture on your cheek,
what will you say that is? A flake
of snow, melting? No, no, it
flows from your anguished heart.
BRAND: Agnes, my own, my wife, let us both
be steadfast, even unto death.
Out there I was a chosen man
indeed. I was God's champion.

While, in mid-fjord, the boat
laboured, sea-drenched I fought.
The tiller strained in my hand
yet steadied as it strained.
Eight souls froze at the oars
like corpses on their biers.
The mast groaned, cordage clashed, flung
loose on the wind. Our seams were sprung.
The canvas blew to shreds,
whipped to leeward. The seabirds'
cries were drowned. Through darkness I saw
cliff-falls, cataracts of snow,
crash down upon the rocks.
And all this while, He who makes
storm and calm held me to His will.
Through sea-howl I heard Him call.

AGNES: How easy it is to wage war
on the elements, and to dare
all. How hard it seems to wait
as I must, so very quiet,
while life ticks by; and be at home
to all the visitings of time;
and hear the ceaseless sparrow-
flutterings of sorrow
in the eaves of the heart's house.
I long to be of use
in the great world. I dare not
remember, cannot forget.
Know me for what I am.

BRAND: Agnes, for shame, for shame!
How can you think to scorn
your life's work, its true crown:
my helpmate and my wife?
Listen, and I'll reveal
strange mercies wrought from grief.
Sometimes, Agnes, my eyes fill
with tears of gratitude.
I think that I see God,

so close. As never before
I greet Him face to face,
feel His fatherly care.
Then I desire to cast
myself on His breast,
weeping in His embrace.

AGNES: And may He always appear
so to you, Brand. Fathers forgive.
It is tyrants who rave.

BRAND: O Agnes, you must ever fear
to question Him. Never presume
to turn your face away from Him.
I am the servant of that Lord.
I am the warrior with the sword
of righteousness. Your gentle hands
shall soothe and heal my wounds.
Agnes, embrace your task!

AGNES: Everything that you ask
of me seems too heavy to bear.
I'm so weary I can scarcely hear
what you say. Thoughts ravel my mind
without beginning or end.
I gaze at my own life
almost with disbelief.
My dearest, let me grieve
and I may learn to live
and serve you, purged of sorrow
at last . . . I don't know.
Brand, while you were away,
I saw my little boy
again, I saw him! He came
smiling into my room.
He looked, as once he did,
bright-eyed and rosy-cheeked.
He came towards my bed
as though to be cradled and rocked
in my arms. It made my blood run cold.

BRAND: Agnes!

AGNES: I knew that he'd turned
    to ice, out there in the icy ground.
BRAND: Believe me, Agnes, our child
    has been gathered to God,
    he is in Paradise.
    It is a corpse that lies
    out there under the snow.
AGNES [*shrinking away from him*]:
    Why do you tear and prod
    at the wound, make the blood flow?
    The body and the soul
    go down into the soil
    together. Together they rise up
    out of our mortal sleep.
    I cannot discriminate
    like you; I cannot tell them apart.
    To me they are as one,
    soul, body . . . my son.
BRAND: Many an old wound shall
    bleed to make you well.
AGNES: Stay by me in my need,
    Brand; for I'll not be led
    against my will. Please try
    to be gentle; speak gently.
    Your voice is like a storm
    when you drive a soul to choose
    its own poor martyrdom.
    Is there no gentler voice
    that says to pain, 'Be still',
    no song that greets the light,
    no gentleness at all?
    Your God, I see Him sit
    just like some grim seigneur
    in His stronghold. I fear
    to irritate His gaze
    with my weak woman's cries.
BRAND: It seems, then, you'd prefer
    the God you knew before.

AGNES: Einar's mild God? Never!
  Yet I feel as if I were drawn
  by a longing for clear, pure air
  where it's drawing towards dawn.
  Your visions, your new realms,
  your calling, your iron will,
  everything looms, overwhelms,
  threatens me, like the cliff
  that would bury us if it fell
  or the fjord that cuts us off
  from the world. Brand! Brand! Such
  pain! And for what? Your little church
  that crouches under the rock
  like a mouse from a hawk?

BRAND [struck]:
  Again, again, that thought,
  like a tremor of air. What
  makes you speak so? Why do you say
  the church is too small?

AGNES [shaking her head sorrowfully]:
                            How can I
  give reasons? How do I know?
  How do the winds blow,
  how does a scent travel
  on the air? Must I unravel
  everything that goes through my mind?
  It is enough that I understand.
  Call it instinct, if you will.
  Brand, your church is too small.

BRAND: 'The young shall see visions and the old
  dream dreams.' What mysteries unfold,
  my Agnes! Even she I met
  wandering on the mountain height
  in madness froze me with that call:
  'The church is hideous and small, small.'
  Whether she knew of what she spoke
  I cannot tell: but the womenfolk
  echo her, murmuring all the time,

as though possessed of the same dream,
visionary things, things yet unknown,
strange intimations of new Zion.
Dear angel of my destiny,
you bless and guide me on my way.
The church *is* small, I see it now.
It shall be built anew,
and the Lord God shall enter in
to His own temple once again.

AGNES: From this time forward, let it seem
as if a wide deserted sea
lay blank between my grief and me.
I shall decide upon a tomb
and bury the dead hopes of life;
and make each mirrored citadel
vanish as in a fairy-tale.
I'll be your dedicated wife.

BRAND: Agnes, the road leads on.

AGNES: You sound so cold and stern,
even now.

BRAND: It is God
who speaks, not I.

AGNES: You've said
that He is merciful
to those who faint and fall,
if they'll but persevere.
          [*She turns to leave.*]

BRAND: Agnes, must you go?

AGNES [*smiling*]:
It's Christmas Eve, my dear,
and I have things to do.
Last Christmas you chided me
a little for my extravagance:
a lit candle in every sconce,
and shining glass and greenery,
the room alive with laughter's song
and all the gifts that love could bring.
The candles shall be lit again;

we'll deck the tree; do what we can
to keep our Christmas, and rejoice
inwardly in the silent house.
If God should stare into this room
tonight, Brand, I need feel no shame.
I've watched and prayed, wiped every trace
of grief, each tear smudge, from my face,
you see; all gone now! I would meet
Him with a truly chastened heart.

    [BRAND *pulls her towards him in an embrace; then*
    abruptly lets her go.]

BRAND: Go, light the candles. There, hush!

AGNES [*smiling sorrowfully*]:
And let the church be built all new
and bright by the spring thaw.
Let us make that our Christmas wish!

    [*Exit.*]

BRAND [*gazing after her*]:
Help me, O help me, God,
to spare her more agony.
It's like watching her die
in martyrdom's slow flame.
What else must I perform
that your law may be satisfied,
lex talionis, your hawk
that will swoop down and take
the heart out of her?
Let me be the martyr,
not her. Dear God! Haven't I faith
and strength, and will, enough for both?
Let her devoted love suffice.
Remit, O Lord, remit the sacrifice.

    [*There is a knock at the door. The* MAYOR *enters.*]

MAYOR: Well, here I am, d'you see,
come to eat humble pie!
Sir, I'm a beaten man,
beaten and trampled on!

BRAND: You, Mayor?

MAYOR: I'm not joking.
   I tried to send you packing.
   I admit, I said at the time,
   I said, there isn't room
   for both of us. I was right,
   no shadow of a doubt,
   no doubt at all. Yet here
   I am with my white flag.
   My friend, I come to beg.
   There's a new spirit abroad
   in the region, praise God,
   suddenly it's everywhere –
   but not mine: *yours*,
   Pastor. The war's
   over. Stop the fight.
   Now, let's shake hands on that!

BRAND: Between the two of us
   the strife can never cease,
   for spiritual war
   is endless; must be waged
   however bruised and scourged
   and desolate we are.

MAYOR: Don't try to win a fight
   if it pays you to lose:
   I call that compromise.

BRAND: Though you deride God's law,
   nothing can make black white!

MAYOR: My dear man, you can holler,
   'White as the driven snow',
   till you're blue in the face.
   If our wise populace
   prefers snow to be black,
   then black it is. Hard luck!

BRAND: And what's your favourite colour?

MAYOR: Mine's a nice in-between
   delicate shade of grey.
   I've told you, I'm humane.
   I meet people half-way.

I don't gallop head-on
against opinion.
I let the crowd decide,
run with the multitude.
You're the crowd's candidate,
it seems; so here's *my* vote.
I've had to shelve my plans
for new ditches and drains,
for new jetties and roads,
and Lord knows what besides.
Still, if that's the game,
I'll play it. 'Bide your time,'
I tell myself, 'and smile.
Hang on to fortune's wheel
like the grim death. Your turn
always comes round again.'

BRAND: There speaks the 'public spirit'
in essence, Mayor. It
seems, then, that greed, if shrewd,
can pass as zeal-for-good.

MAYOR: That's not how it is at all!
I've lived a life of real
self-sacrificing labour,
a man who's served his neighbour
more than he's served himself.
I spit on this world's pelf.
But surely, surely, it's fair,
isn't it, Minister,
that honesty and good sense
should gain some recompense?
When all's been said you can't
let your own kith and kin
go hungry. I've got daughters.
I must think of their futures.
You know what that can mean.
Chewing on the ideal
won't get you a square meal
and it won't pay the rent.

He who says otherwise
doesn't know what life is!

BRAND: What will you do now?

MAYOR: Build.

BRAND: Did you say build?

MAYOR: I did.
I'll serve the nation's need
as I served it of old.
I'll dazzle people's eyes
with some great enterprise.
I'll be cock of the roost,
I'll strut upon my post.
By God, you'll hear me crow
pro bono publico!
My new election cry
is 'Down with poverty!'

BRAND: You mean to stamp it out?

MAYOR: I've a much better thought.
Well, come on, use your wits!
What am I planning? It's
my 'hygienic edifice',
a bargain at the price!
A workhouse and a gaol
under the same roof;
perfectly clean and safe
and economical.
Then, having made a start,
I'll add an extra wing
built to accommodate
wassail, that sort of thing,
banquets and lantern-slide
lectures, what you will:
the Patriots' Pledge hall.

BRAND: There may be some need
for the things you name –
but there is one thing more,
with a far higher claim.

MAYOR: A madhouse, to be sure!

But who would foot the bill?

BRAND: Well, if you need to house
    your madmen, why not use
    the Patriots' Pledge hall?
    It would be suitable.

MAYOR [*delighted*]:
    The Patriots' Pledge hall
    a madhouse all the time –
    O Pastor, what a scheme!
    How could it ever fail?
    We'll soon have crime and sin
    and madness all crammed in;
    then we'll cram in the poor
    and lock and bolt the door.

BRAND: You need money, you said.

MAYOR: I think that puts the case
    fairly enough. I've tried.
    Cash for a worthy cause
    seems very hard to find.
    A well-placed word or two
    from 't'People's' Pastor Brand
    would turn the tide. You know
    I shan't forget a friend.

BRAND: I know I'm being bribed.

MAYOR: Couldn't it be described
    as the best way of healing
    old wounds, and that sad breach
    between us, from which each
    of us, I know, has suffered,
    since we're both men of feeling.

BRAND: *Suffered*, did you say?

MAYOR: Of course, of course, the boy . . .
    I trust that you'll accept
    condolences as offered.
    You seemed, though, so imbued
    with Christian fortitude
    I took it that the worst
    excess of grief had passed.

I came because I'd hoped . . .
BRAND: You've hoped and schemed in vain.
I also plan to build.
MAYOR: To steal my master plan –
well, I must say, that's bold!
BRAND: You say so? Look out there –
[*Points out of the window*]
no, there; what do you see?
MAYOR: Not much, if you ask me!
That old barn with a tilt?
Look, I don't understand . . .
BRAND: The *church*. Mayor, I intend
the *church* shall be rebuilt
on a grander scale.
MAYOR: But – dammit – that's *my* style.
Just leave things as they are,
I'll make it worth your while.
Why pull the old place down?
BRAND: I have said: it is small.
MAYOR: Small? But I've never seen
it more than half-full.
BRAND: There's no space, no air,
for the spirit to soar!
MAYOR [*aside*]:
If he goes on like this,
he'll need the services
of the madhouse himself.
[*Aloud*]
Pastor, take my advice,
leave the church to the mice,
I beg you, on behalf
of the whole neighbourhood.
I rise to the defence
of our inheritance.
An architectural gem
destroyed for a mere whim?
No, it can't be allowed!
BRAND: I'll build God's house with my

    own substance; dedicate
    every last farthing-bit
    out of my legacy.
MAYOR: Well! I'm thunderstruck!
    I can't believe our luck,
    I can't, truly I can't!
    Riches without stint,
    a great gold, glittering stream –
    tell me it's not a dream!
BRAND: I've made up my mind,
    long ago, to renounce
    that cursed inheritance.
MAYOR: I'm with you heart and soul,
    I'm filled with purest zeal.
    Onward then! Hand in hand!
    Here's to our enterprise –
    how's that for a surprise?
    I dare to think that fate
    has brought me here tonight.
    I even dare to think
    that you have me to thank
    and that your miracle
    is mine after all.
BRAND: Destroy that 'hallowed fane'
    out there? Why, it's a shrine!
MAYOR: H'm, that's as may be.
    I must say, viewed from here
    now that the moon's so bright,
    it's exceedingly shabby.
    The weathercock and the spire,
    they're in a dreadful state!
    And the roof and the walls,
    ugly beyond belief,
    a mere hotchpotch of styles.
    Is that moss on the roof?
BRAND: And if the populace
    cried out, as with one voice,
    'Leave the old church alone!',

what would you do then?
MAYOR: I'll show you what I'd do.
   I know a trick or two
   for rousing the nation.
   I'll canvass, agitate,
   start a petition.
   If that doesn't succeed
   in whipping up the crowd,
   I'll tear the place apart
   myself; and I'll be brisk
   about it, even if
   I have to set my wife
   and daughters to the task
   of demolition.
BRAND: Well, Mayor, you've changed your tune,
   slightly, since we began!
MAYOR: A liberal education
   rids one of prejudice.
   Good heavens, how time flies!
   I must be on my way,
   I must indeed. Good-bye,
   Pastor, good-bye.
              [*Takes his hat*]
                        I'm
   hot in pursuit of crime.
BRAND: What crime?
MAYOR: Early today
   right on the parish bounds,
   a gypsy tribe – such fiends
   they are! I took the lot.
   What do you think of that?
   They're all snugly tied up
   and under lock and key.
   Well, not all. Two or three
   managed to escape.
BRAND: And this is the season
   of peace and goodwill!
MAYOR: All the more reason

to clap them in gaol;
they bring trouble and strife.
And yet, they've cause enough.
In an odd sort of way
they belong to the parish;
to you, even; though 'Perish
the thought,' I hear you say.
Look here, do you like
riddles? Here's a joke.
Decipher this rune:
Not of your kith nor kin
but of your origin.
Why were we born?

BRAND: Where is the answer?

MAYOR: Not too hard,
surely? You must have heard
many and many a time,
about that lad who came
from yonder, from the West;
as clever as a priest
or four priests put together,
for all that he was poor.
This lad loved your mother.
She'd property of her own,
a few acres of stone,
wouldn't be wooed nor wed,
not she. Showed him the door,
she did. And that put paid
to *his* hopes. He went half
out of his mind with grief,
half out of his mind.
But there it is. In the end
he took another lass,
a gypsy she was,
and fathered a whole brood
out of her gypsy blood.
Those imps of sin and shame,
they're his, some of them.

Oh yes, we pay the fine
for his fine goings-on.
Why, one of his brats
even gets clothed and fed
out of the parish rates!

BRAND: Of course . . .

MAYOR: That troll-wench, Gerd.

BRAND: Now I begin to see . . .

MAYOR: A right riddle-me-ree.
Who'd believe it? A lad
goes silly in the head
because of your mother,
how many years ago?
Now here you are. And I've
to waste all Christmas Eve
chasing his sons and daughters
for miles across the snow
in this foul weather.

BRAND: But whips and fetters . . . !

MAYOR: Pastor, don't waste your time.
They're sunk in sin and crime.
Shove them behind bars.
Let charity go shares
with Satan in this world.
Old Nick mustn't catch cold.

BRAND: Surely you had a plan
to house the destitute?

MAYOR: My plan has been withdrawn
in favour of your own.

BRAND: But if you had my support . . .

MAYOR [*smiling*]:
Well, you have changed your tune!
   [*Pats his shoulder*]
What's done can't be undone.
Life has its rewards.
And now I must be off.
Merry Christmas. Regards
to your good lady wife!

[*Exit.*]

BRAND [*a brooding silence; then*]:
Atonement without end,
guilt with guilt intertwined,
deadly contagion
of sin breeding with sin;
deed issuing from deed
hideously inbred.
Right ceasing to be right
even as one stares at it!

[*Goes to the window and looks out for a long while*]
The innocent must atone.
Therefore God took my son.
And the hurt soul of Gerd
pays for my mother's greed.
And it was Gerd's voice
that drove me to my choice.
Each generation
of us hunted down
by that just God, who is
terrible to praise.
The sacrificial will
is what redeems man's soul!
Even in those darkest days
when grief and dread possessed
me; and I saw that our child slept
too deeply ever to be kissed
awake; even then my prayers
never ceased. Even then,
amid all that pain,
I was held, still and rapt
as though by some serene
music, steadily drawing near,
carried upon the air.
But was I then restored?
Did I speak with God?
Did He, then, turn His gaze
on this grief-stricken house?

The 'efficacy of prayer' —
what does that mean:
that prayer is a talisman
fingered by rich and poor,
a superstitious fear
that goes justly unheard,
an indiscriminate
battering at the gate
of the silent Word?
O Agnes, it's so dark!

> [AGNES *opens the door and enters with the lighted candles
> in festive holders; a clear radiance suffuses the room.*]

AGNES: The Christmas candles, look!

BRAND: Ah! How the candles gleam!

AGNES: Have I been long?

BRAND: No, no.

AGNES: It's like ice in this room.
You must be frozen, too.

BRAND: No.

AGNES: Why are you too proud
to show me that you need
comfort? Why, my dear?

> [*She puts wood in the stove.*]

BRAND: Too proud?

> [*He walks up and down.*]

AGNES [*softly to herself as she decorates the room*]:
               The candles here,
so. He sat in his chair
and laughed, and tried to touch,
and said it was the sun.
The sun! He was such
a happy little boy.

> [*Moves a candlestick slightly*]

And a whole year has gone;
and the candle shines clear
over the place where he lies.
And he can see us
if he chooses to come

and gaze in, quietly,
at the still candle-flame.
But now the window blurs
with breath-mist, like tears.
    [*She wipes the window.*]
BRAND [*slowly, following her with his eyes*]:
When will the sea of grief
subside and let her rest?
AGNES [*to herself*]:
How clear it is; as if
this room had opened out;
as if the earth were not
iron-hard and icy cold
but soft, warm as a nest
where our sleeping child
can lie snug and secure.
BRAND: What are you doing there?
AGNES: Why, a dream; it was
a dream.
BRAND: Snares are laid
cruelly, in dreams, Agnes.
Close the shutters.
AGNES: Brand,
I beg you, don't be hard.
BRAND: Close them.
AGNES: There. It's done.
    [*Pulls the shutters to*]
My dreams will never offend
God, of that I'm sure.
He'll not grudge me the pure
waters of consolation.
BRAND: Grudge? Of course He'll not grudge
the . . .! He's a lenient judge
if you bow down to Him
and if you grease His palm,
practise idolatry
a little, on the sly.
AGNES [*bursting into tears*]:

How much . . . oh how much more
will you make me endure?

BRAND: I have said: if you give
less than everything,
you may as well fling
your gift into the sea.

AGNES: All that I had, I gave.
There's nothing left of me.

BRAND: I have said: there's no end
to what God can demand
of us.

AGNES: I'm destitute,
so I've nothing to fear.

BRAND: Every sinful desire,
each longing, each regret . . .

AGNES: You've forgotten my heart's root!
Sacrifice that as well!
Rip *that* out! Rip it out!

BRAND: And if you grieve at all,
if you begrudge your loss,
then God will refuse
everything you have given.

AGNES [*shuddering*]:
Is this your way to Heaven?
It's hard and desolate.

BRAND: Steep, narrow and straight;
and the will is able!

AGNES: But mercy's path . . . ?

BRAND: Is hewn
from sacrificial stone.

AGNES [*staring in front of her, shaken*]:
Now I know what the Bible
means; now I can fathom,
as never before, those grim
words.

BRAND: Which words?

AGNES: 'He who sees
Jehovah's face, dies.'

BRAND [*throwing his arms around her and pressing her close*]:
  Hide your eyes!
AGNES: Hide me!
BRAND [*letting her go*]:   No.
AGNES: You are in torment too.
BRAND: I love you.
AGNES: Your love is hard.
BRAND: Too hard?
AGNES: Don't ask me that.
  I follow where you lead.
BRAND: You think I drew you out
  of Einar's trivial dance
  unthinkingly, or by chance?
  Or that for nothing
  I broke every plaything?
  Or that for less than all
  I bound you to obey
  the unconditional
  demand for sacrifice?
  Woe befall us, I say,
  if ever that were so!
  Agnes, you were called
  by God to be my wife.
  And I dare to demand
  your *all*, your whole life.
AGNES: I am yours; I am bound.
  Ask of me what you will,
  but don't, don't go away.
BRAND: My dear one, I must.
  I must find rest and peace.
  And soon I shall build
  my great church.
AGNES: My little
  church crumbled to dust.
BRAND: The heart's idolatry
  must be so destroyed!
        [*Embraces her as if in agony*]
  Peace be with you, for then

peace is with me and mine.

AGNES: May I move the shutter aside,
just a little? Let me, Brand, let
me.

BRAND [*in the doorway*]:
No.

[*He goes into his room.*]

AGNES: Shut out, everything shut
away. Where is my hope of Heaven?
I cannot seek oblivion;
or touch his hand and weep;
or rend my body to escape
from breathing this fierce air.
There's no release from fear,
the solitude that we call God.

[*Listens at* BRAND's *door*]

His voice moves on; so loud
he cannot hear, and never will.
High above grief the lords of Yule
bring tidings to another world
than mine. Even the Holy Child
has turned away. He smiles on those
with the most cause to sing His praise,
fortune's good children, who enjoy
His love like any longed-for toy.

[*Approaches the window cautiously*]

But if I disobeyed
Brand, if I opened wide
the shutters, all this light,
flooding the darkness, might
comfort my little son
out there under the stone.
No, no, he's not dead.
Tonight the child is freed,
for this is the Child's feast.
But what if Brand knows best?
What if I now do wrong?
O little one, take wing!

This house of ours is sealed
against you, my own child.
Your father turned the lock
against you. Love, go back,
go back to Heaven and play.
I dare not disobey
Brand. Say that you saw
your father's sorrow –
how can you understand,
my darling? Let's pretend
it was his grief that made
this wreath out of leaves,
so pretty! Tell them, 'He grieves.'

[*Listens, considers and shakes her head*]

No! You are locked outside,
my dear, by stronger powers
than doors or shutter bars.
Fierce spiritual flame
is needed to consume
their strength, make the vaults crack
open, the barriers break,
and the great prison door
swing loose upon the air.
I must purge the whole world
with my own sacrifice, child,
before I see you again.
And I shall become stone
myself, struggling to fill
the bottomless pit
of Brand's absolute.
There's still a little time,
though; time for festival;
and though it's far removed
from Christmas as it was,
I'll be glad of what is,
give thanks for what I have –
the treasures that I saved
from the wreck of my life's good,

all of them, all of them!

> [*She kneels down by the chest of drawers, opens a drawer and takes out various things. At the same moment* BRAND *opens the door and is about to speak to her, but when he sees what she is doing he stops and remains standing there.* AGNES *does not see him.*]

BRAND [*softly*]:
This hovering over the grave,
this playing in the garden of the dead!

AGNES: Why, here's the robe and shawl
he wore to his christening;
and here's a bundle full
of baby things. Dear Heaven,
every pretty thing
he was ever given!
Oh, and I dressed him
in these mittens and scarf,
and this little coat,
to keep him warm and safe
when he went out
in spring for the first time.
And the things I prepared
all ready for the road,
that journey of his life
which was never begun.
And when I took them off
him, and put them away,
I felt so utterly
weary and full of pain.

BRAND [*clenching his hands in pain*]:
O God, spare me this!
How can I condemn
these last idolatries
of hers? She clings to them.

AGNES: Tear stains, here and here . . .
like pearls on a holy
relic. I see the halo
of inescapable choice

shine now, terribly clear.
This robe of sacrifice
was his and is mine.
I am a rich woman.

[*There is a sharp knock on the house door.* AGNES
turns round with a cry and, in doing so, sees BRAND.
The door is flung open and a GYPSY WOMAN, *in
ragged clothes, comes in with a child in her arms.*]

GYPSY WOMAN: Share them with me, you rich lady!
AGNES: But you are richer than I.
GYPSY WOMAN: Mouthfuls of pretty words.
Rich folk, you're all the same.
Show us some good deeds!
BRAND: Tell me, why have you come?
GYPSY WOMAN: Tell you? Not I! Talk to a priest?
I'd as lief walk the storm again
as hear you ranting about sin,
and how us poor folk are accurst.
I'd as lief run until I die
and leave my bones out on the skerry
as look you in the eye, you black
man full of hell-fire talk!
BRAND [*softly*]:
That voice, that face . . . the woman
stands there like an omen,
like a visitor from the dead.
AGNES: Rest, rest. If you are cold,
come to the fire. If the child
is hungry, he shall be fed.
GYPSY WOMAN: Can't stay, lady; can't rest.
House and home, they're for the likes
of you, not for us gypsies' sakes.
Folk long since turned us out-o'-door
for a bit lodging on the moor
or in the woods, as best we can,
bedded on rock and the rough whin.
We come and go, and we go fast,
wi' lawyer-men, just like dogs,

howling and snapping at our legs.
Won't let us rest, yon lawyer-men,
clinking up close wi' whip and chain.
BRAND: Be quiet, woman. Here, you're safe.
GYPSY WOMAN: Safe? Here? Crammed in wi' walls and
    roof?
Nay, master, nay; we're better far
to wander through the bitter air.
But gi'e us something for the brat.
His own brother stole the clout
o' rags that he was swaddled in.
Look, lady, look, his naked skin
all white wi' frost and blue wi' cold!
BRAND: Woman, I beg you, set this child
free from the path of death-in-life.
He shall be cherished; every stain
of blood and guilt shall be washed off.
GYPSY WOMAN: Why, it was you folk cast him out,
it was, and now I curse you for it.
Where do you think, then, he was born?
Not in a bed! His mother took
bad at the bottom of a syke.
Christened he was, wi' a dab o' slush
and a charcoal stick out of the ash;
a swig o' gin his comforter.
And when we lugged him out of her,
who cursed him and his puny whine?
His fathers – ay, he'd more than one!
BRAND: Agnes?
AGNES: Yes.
BRAND: What must you do?
AGNES: Give them to *her*? O Brand! No!
GYPSY WOMAN: Oh yes, rich lady, all you have!
Ragged sark or silken weave,
nowt's too rotten or too good
if I can wrap it round his hide.
Like as not he'll soon be dead.
At least he'll die wi' his limbs thawed.

BRAND: The choice, Agnes! Hear the call,
   harsh and inescapable!
GYPSY WOMAN: You've plenty. You could dress your bairn
   ten times over. Look at mine!
   Spare us a shroud, for pity's sake!
BRAND: The demand, Agnes! Hear it speak,
   absolute and imperative!
GYPSY WOMAN: Gi'e us that, lady, gi'e us that!
AGNES: Don't you dare, gypsy! Desecrate,
   would you, my babe, my love,
   and all these pretty things?
BRAND: Hush, child.
   He's dead. I say: he died in vain
   if you lose faith. Then the road leads
   nowhere but to the threshold
   of the grave.
AGNES [*brokenly*]:
               Thy will be done.
   With my last strength I'll tear out
   my heart, trample it underfoot.
   Share, then! Put my 'superfluous
   riches' to some better use.
GYPSY WOMAN: Give it here! Give it here!
BRAND: Agnes, did you say share?
AGNES: Yes. I beg you, let me be killed
   now, and not be made to yield
   any more. Give her what she needs,
   half, even. Let me keep the rest.
BRAND: Then half would have sufficed,
   would it not, for your own son?
AGNES: Here, gypsy, take the christening-
   robe, and the scarf, and the silken
   bonnet; take everything
   that will keep out the cold.
GYPSY WOMAN: Gi'e us, then.
BRAND: Agnes, are you sure
   that's all?
AGNES: Here's the shirt he wore

on the day he died. I called
it his robe of martyrdom.

GYPSY WOMAN: It'll do. Is that the lot,
lady? Right, then; I'll flit –
after I've seen to him.
[*Exit.*]

AGNES: Demand on top of demand –
is it reasonable, Brand?

BRAND: Did you give with heart and soul,
without bitterness at all?

AGNES: No!

BRAND: No? Then you have flung away
your gifts, and you are still not free.
[*He prepares to leave.*]

AGNES: Brand!

BRAND: Yes?

AGNES: Oh, Brand, I lied!
Forgive me, for I hid
the last, my very last
relic. Hadn't you guessed?

BRAND: Well?

AGNES [*taking a folded child's cap from her bosom*]:
            Look, one thing remains.

BRAND: His cap?

AGNES: Marked with the stains
of my tears, and his cold fever sweat;
and kept close-hidden at my heart!

BRAND: Worship your idols, then.
[*He prepares to leave.*]

AGNES: No, wait!

BRAND: For what?

AGNES: You know for what.
[*She holds out the cap.*]

BRAND [*coming towards her without taking it*]:
Without regret?

AGNES: Without regret!

BRAND: Very well, then. His cap,
give it to me. The woman

is still there, sitting on the step.
>   [*Exit.*]

AGNES: Everything's gone now, everything's lost.

>   [AGNES *stands for some moments completely still; grad-*
>   *ually the expression on her face is transformed into pure*
>   *radiant joy.* BRAND *returns; she goes exultantly to meet*
>   *him, throws her arms around his neck and cries out*]

O Brand, O Brand, at last I'm free
of everything that drew me to the dust!

BRAND: Agnes!

AGNES: The darkness has gone,
and the ghosts, and the nightmares,
the leaden fears that weighed me down.
And I know that victory
is certain, if the will endures.
The mists have all dispersed
and all the clouds have passed
away; and at the end of night
I see the first faint rosy light
of dawn. And I'll not be afraid,
or hurt, or weep to hear the word
'death', or the sound of my child's name.
I know that Heaven is his home.
I have overcome grief,
and even the grave itself
yields, and our little Alf
shines in his immortality,
his face radiant with joy
just as it was in life.
If my strength were a thousandfold,
If my voice were like that
of a great choir, if I could
be heard in Heaven, I'd not
plead, now, for his return.
How wondrous is our God,
how infinite His resource
in making His ways known
to men. Through the sacrifice

of my child, through the command
'Atone, and again, atone!',
my soul has been restored.
God gives, takes back, His own.
I was purged by ordeal.
You guided my hand,
you battled for my soul,
though your grim silent heart
cried out even as you fought.
Now it is you who stand
in the valley of the choice,
you who must bear the cross,
the terrible burthen
of all or nothing.

BRAND: You speak in riddles, Agnes. It
is finished, all that agony.

AGNES: Beloved, you forget:
'Whoever looks on God shall die.'

BRAND [*shrinking back*]:
Dearest! What terrors wake
in my heart when you speak
like that! Be strong!
I could let all things go,
every earthly good; everything,
everything but you!

AGNES: Choose. You stand where the roads cross.
Quench this light new-lit in me,
choke the springs of divine grace,
allow me my idolatry.
The gypsy woman, call her back,
give me back the things she took.
Let me clutch them, weak and craven,
blindly ignorant of Heaven.
Clip the wing-feathers of my soul,
fetter me at wrist and heel
with the constraints of each bleak day,
and then I'll be as I once was,
a prisoner of mortality.

Choose. You stand where the roads cross.

BRAND: All would be lost if I
weakened, if I chose the way
you point to . . . but . . . far from this place,
beyond the memories
of all this bitter grief,
my Agnes, we shall find that life
and light are one.

AGNES: But you are bound,
by your own choice and His demand.
You must remain; must be the guide
of many souls in their great need.
Choose. You stand where the roads cross.

BRAND: No choice . . . I have no choice.

AGNES [*throwing her arms round his neck*]:
I give you thanks for all I have,
and for your own dear love
to me, poor, weary, stumbling one.
My eyes are heavy, and the mist
gathers, and I must rest.

BRAND: Beloved, sleep. Your work is done.

AGNES: Yes, the day labour, the soul's fight,
are finished. Now the night-
candle shall burn with steady flame
as my thoughts rest on Him.
[*Exit.*]

BRAND [*clenching his hands against his breast*]:
Be steadfast, O my soul,
for in the loss of all
this world's good lies our gain.
We, at the end, are blest
and all that we have lost
is ours for evermore. Amen.

ACT FIVE

*A year and a half later. The new church stands ready and decorated for the
consecration ceremony. The river is close by. It is early misty morning. The
church organ can be heard playing softly. A crowd is murmuring in the distance.
The* SEXTON *is hanging up garlands outside the church. After a few moments, enter* SCHOOLMASTER.

SCHOOLMASTER: Sexton? Up with the lark!
SEXTON: I'm never one to shirk;
    not like some, Schoolmaster.
    Pass me that bunting.
SCHOOLMASTER: They're
    making a dreadful din
    round at the Pastor's house.
    Whatever's going on?
SEXTON: They're putting up a plaque,
    gold-plated if you please!
SCHOOLMASTER: Well, Brand's drawing the crowds,
    no doubt of that! The fjord's
    already white with sails.
    They're flocking in from miles . . .
SEXTON: He's chivvied folk awake,
    has Brand. But for what?
    In the old pastor's time
    everything was calm,
    year in and year out.
    Now it's all rage and strife.
SCHOOLMASTER: That's life, Sexton, that's life!
    That's what it takes to build
    'the brave new world'!

SEXTON: Maybe. But I feel lost.
　　This can't be for the best.
　　Are you and I asleep?
　　Are we both out of step?
SCHOOLMASTER: Others slept. We had work
　　to do. And then they woke
　　and said we'd had our day,
　　just like they always say.
SEXTON: But you've just sung the praise
　　of this newfangledness!
SCHOOLMASTER: 'When in Rome', Sexton, 'when
　　in Rome'! You've heard the Dean.
　　It's not for us to march
　　contrary to the Church,
　　the spiritual élite.
　　We're servants of the state.
　　But, Sexton, man to man,
　　I'm all for discipline.
　　We live in troubled times.
　　Why should we fan the flames?
　　There's no reason to feed
　　every faction and feud.
SEXTON: Brand, now; he's in the thick
　　of things . . .
SCHOOLMASTER: Up to his neck!
　　But then, of course, he's shrewd
　　and very hard to catch.
　　He knows the common herd,
　　he's got the common touch.
　　If he says, 'I've got plans',
　　no one asks him, 'For what?' –
　　far-sighted citizens
　　all clutching at his coat
　　and tagging at his heels
　　up hill, down dale, blind fools!
SEXTON: You've been in politics,
　　you're wise to all such tricks;
　　you know the public mind.

SCHOOLMASTER: This is the promised land,
    but who's it promised to?
    Will someone tell me that?
    I'd really like to know.
SEXTON: Listen!
SCHOOLMASTER: What's that?
SEXTON: That sound!
SCHOOLMASTER: Strange . . . the organ . . .
SEXTON: That's Brand
    for sure! Only Brand plays
    like that; sometimes whole days
    and nights.
SCHOOLMASTER: He's early.
SEXTON: Late,
    more like. I'll wager he's not
    slept at all. Since he became
    a widower, his soul's been gnawed.
    Sometimes, I think, he grows half-mad
    with grieving for his wife and son.
    And then he plays some endless tune
    as though, in every note you hear,
    they cry and he's their comforter,
    or he weeps and they comfort him.
SCHOOLMASTER: Ah, if only one dared
    let one's soul be stirred . . .
    and if one weren't constrained
    by rules of every kind . . . !
    Right-thinking men must take
    a stronger stand. 'Lord, make
    me worthy to be mayor'
    is no ignoble prayer.
    That fire at the Mayor's house,
    remember? The flames rose
    and danced above the roof
    and roared like Satan's laugh.
    And the Mayor's wife! Such screams,
    as though she'd seen Hell's flames
    and seen Old Nick and all

agog for the Mayor's soul!
'Stay clear! Let it all go!'
she begged. He wouldn't, though.
That good and faithful man,
he had the strength of ten,
saved every last receipt,
the archives, all complete!
The Mayor – he's my ideal
official: heart and soul
a mayor; inside and out
and tooth and nail, the lot!

SEXTON: Brave deeds and words may seem
old-fashioned, but, like you,
I find that they ring true;
worthy of all esteem!
Folk ought to show respect
for standards, that's a fact.

SCHOOLMASTER: 'The old order must die',
there's a fine rallying cry.
'Feed history to the fire',
you hear that everywhere.
When they saw fit to pull
down the old church and all
that went with it, the custom
of our lives, their trim and form . . .

SEXTON: I was there, Schoolmaster!
A great groan rent the air.
Folk were terrified!
Some had a look of shame;
some knew the fear of God,
I'd say, for the first time.

SCHOOLMASTER: For a while they felt bound
to the old in a thousand
ways. Then they took stock
of the new building work.
Dazzled by what they saw,
with a good deal of awe-
struck relish, one might say,

they awaited the great day.
Then, even as the spire climbed
higher, they grew alarmed.
Well, the great day has come.

SEXTON [*pointing to one side*]:
Lord bless us, what a swarm
of people! And that murmuring sound . . .
the sea under a rising wind . . .

SCHOOLMASTER: The spirit of the age! It stirs
the hearts of men with strange new fears,
with the deep tremors of the time;
as though a voice had summoned them.

SEXTON: I think . . . no, it's absurd . . .

SCHOOLMASTER: What is? . . .

SEXTON: That we've been stirred
more than we dare admit.

SCHOOLMASTER: What nonsense! Do be quiet,
Sexton! We're both grown men,
not silly maids at school.
Discipline! Discipline!
[*Exit to one side.*]

SEXTON [*to himself*]:
Pah! Sexton, you're a fool;
you'll blether yourself sick.
'I think that we've been stirred . . .'
Suppose the Dean had heard!
What *was* it that I saw . . .?
Agh, I don't want to know!
Idle hands, idle talk . . .
[*Exit on the other side. The organ is suddenly heard
very loudly, and the playing ends with a shattering dis-
cord. Shortly afterwards* BRAND *comes out.*]

BRAND: What have I made? Not music, not
music! Cries wrung from music's throat!
Splayed chords of discord, a groan
rising in the place of praise, the organ
stormed, faltered; as if the Lord sat
in the empty choir, raging and quiet,

rebuking with His presence the voice
of thanksgiving and sacrifice.
'Come, let us rebuild the Lord's house',
how splendid that sounded! Promise
like fulfilment, a temple hall
sacred to the immortal will.
High-arching over the world's woes,
my great church: what a vision it was!
O Agnes, if you hadn't died,
things would be different indeed.
Heaven and home were near your heart.
You were the laurel of true life.

    [*Notices the preparations for the festival*]
These garlands, flags on every roof,
the people swarming to my house,
I'm scorched and frozen by this praise!
God grant me light, or cast me out
to the oblivion of the pit!

    [*The* MAYOR *enters in full regalia and greets* BRAND
    effusively.]

MAYOR: So the great day is here!
  May I be first to cheer?
  I'm privileged to greet
  a personage so great,
  so honoured, so well-loved,
  I truly feel quite moved.
  What a red-letter day!
  And how do you feel, eh?

BRAND: As though my heart would burst –
  into ashes, or dust.

MAYOR: Come, come, dear sir, come, come!
  I'll not permit such gloom.
  We want your very best
  performance, the true zest,
  thunder and lightning, all
  the trimmings; yes, the full
  range of your repertoire.
  Everyone will be here.

The acoustics are first-class
too, so the Dean says.
The Dean is most impressed!
I also know he praised
the style of architecture
and the size of the structure.
BRAND: Ah, so he's noticed that.
MAYOR: Beg pardon? Noticed what?
BRAND: It seems so very . . . big.
MAYOR: Seems? Is!
An awe-inspiring size!
BRAND: The things for which we've striven
are turned to parodies.
The new paradise?
A big builder's heaven.
MAYOR: Folk here are well content,
so what more could you want?
All right, they're a bit dim.
So let's not worry them
with talk of 'truth' and 'light'.
Truth isn't worth the fright.
Just give them something big
and they're happy: church, pig-
sty, it doesn't matter;
the bigger the better.
BRAND: A finger on the scales
and damn all principles!
MAYOR: For all our sakes, do try
to keep such thoughts at bay.
You've won the silver cup
for good citizenship.
I'll make a stirring speech,
we'll sing the 'Patriots' Song'.
So all's well with the church.
Today let truth go hang!
BRAND: And at your liars' feast
who gives the loyal toast?
MAYOR: There's no call for abuse.

Just let me put the case.
Right now, my lad, you sit
as fortune's favourite.
The final accolade,
that's yours too. You'll be made
a knight, by royal grace,
Knight of the Cross (Third Class).
BRAND: I have my cross right here.
Deprive me if you dare.
You've never understood
my words – not a single word!
You take a metre rule
to measure the sublime
measureless universe,
God's grandeur over all;
visions of fire and ice,
those blazingly supreme
powers that radiate –
the focus, man's own heart!
I can't . . . I can't go on . . .
You speak to them! Explain . . .
        [*He goes up towards the church.*]
MAYOR [*to himself*]:
'Grandeur' indeed! I think
he's mad. Or is he drunk?
        [*Exit.*]
BRAND [*coming down across the open space*]:
Never – not even on
the dark heights – so alone
as here and now, amid
this bleating multitude!
        [*Looks in the direction which the* MAYOR *has taken*]
He crawls, back to his lies
and safe hypocrisies.
O Agnes, O my dear,
unable to endure
the things that I've endured,
I'm lonely and I'm tired.

Here there's no gain, no loss.
Mere total emptiness.
DEAN [*arriving*]:
My dear flock! You poor sheep!
Poor sheep? Tch! A slip
of the tongue. Pastor! I'll
join you! A rehearsal –
my sermon, you understand –
must keep the text in mind.
Our thanks, sir, for the way
you've fought so manfully,
overcome doubt, abuse,
re-edified God's house.
BRAND: I dreamed a church reborn;
a people cleansed, within.
DEAN: Oh, they'll be clean all right.
You'll find they wipe their feet.
A fine church! Resonant!
It echoes every tone –
two for the price of one;
a one-hundred-per-cent
profit. May I repeat
on behalf of the state
and of the diocese,
our gratitude, our praise?
You'll hear many a wing'd word
sung at the festal board
in the mead hall! The luncheon
today. They did mention . . .?
They did? Good! Colleagues of mine,
young up-and-coming men,
most eager to meet you. But
you're as white as a sheet!
BRAND: I've spent my strength; I've failed;
now I'm to be wassailed
by such as you.
DEAN: Overwrought!
Hardly surprising . . . fought

the good fight, alone.
But now that battle's won.
Be cheered by such a day.
Rest in your victory,
revel in your reward.
Just think of it: a crowd
of thousands from the far-
flung regions drawn to hear
you speak, such is your fame!
My colleagues, all of them,
proud to sit at your feet.
And then – the banquet!
Talk of the fatted calf!
The chef's excelled himself.
Lord, what a spread! Tables
groaning with comestibles.
Look, I welcome this chance
to speak in confidence . . .
BRAND: That's right, Dean, turn the rack!
DEAN: Now, now, Pastor, tck, tck! . . .
in confidence, as I've said,
and amity, let me add,
concerning some slight
details to be set right
in your *unique* approach
to matters of the Church.
Put first things first: maintain
custom and precedent.
It saves embarrassment,
or worse, in the long run.
BRAND: I don't think I quite heard . . .
DEAN: The Church fulfils a need.
It's a repository
for the nation's soul,
for praise and glory
and patriot zeal.
It's a bulwark, a base
for true morality,

every good quality.
I'd have said 'treasure-house'
but these are straitened times.
Today, 'good Christian' chimes
best with 'good citizen',
if you see what I mean.
As the state keeps its eyes
fixed on an earthly prize,
so the state church prefers
conformity as the theme
for its own officers.

BRAND: Your words touch the sublime.

DEAN: Let reason lead the way.
Reason can satisfy
two masters at one time
without rebuke or shame.
But don't ask every oaf
you meet, 'Is your soul safe?'
The modern state, young man,
thrives on republican
sentiments: equal rights
and so on; though it hates
real freedom like the plague.
Égalité? Mere *blague*!
But you, with your *quaint* views,
discover avenues,
nooks, crannies, that reveal
we're not equal at all.
The state deals in numbers.
You speak of 'true members
one with another'.
You've caused us some bother.

BRAND: The eagle is brought down;
the goose soars to the sun.

DEAN: Thanks be to God, we're men,
not fowls of the air.
Still, if you must begin
to quote, quote holy writ.

You'll not improve on that.
Genesis to Revelation,
a wealth of quotation
most instructive to hear.
The Tower of Babel,
now there's a parable
to conjure with. It seems
written for our own times:
everyone talking at once,
nobody making sense.
It's obvious you can't
thrive without government.
We all need rules. The odd
man out, defying God,
deserves his thunderbolt.
For what saith Juvenal?
'*Quem Jupiter*, er, *vult*' –
solitude on the brain
can drive a man insane.
Strive for a common goal
or perish, that's the law.

BRAND: That vision Jacob saw
rising from earth to Heaven:
it is for that I have striven!

DEAN: Personal piety!
That's different! When we die,
of course we go to Him.
(In confidence, ahem!)
You talk of Jacob's ladder –
a most uplifting text.
Faith's one thing, life's another.
Try not to get them mixed.
Six days a week we toil,
'our duties to fulfil';
the seventh day, we rest;
piety soothes the breast.
Religion's like high art,
much better kept apart

for those who can commune.
Be sparing with the Word.
Don't scatter it like seed,
or pearls in front of swine.
I know how you must feel,
in love with the ideal,
seeking for some crusade;
but let me be your guide.
Things are seen differently
in the harsh glare of day.
There must be discipline.
Some things are just not done.
We must know where we stand.
I've spoken like a friend.

BRAND: You'll find I don't fit in
to your contrivance, Dean.

DEAN: Tut, tut! tut, tut! You must!
You'll find that we insist:
'Good servant, come up higher . . .'

BRAND: By plunging in the mire!

DEAN: 'The meek shall be exalted' –
now how can that be faulted?

BRAND: Dean, I'm ill-qualified
to serve. Bring out your dead.

DEAN: God help us all, you can't
believe that I would ever . . .

BRAND: Conscript a cadaver?
You would! The man you want,
that focus of your hopes,
is a convenient corpse
down at the mortuary,
a bag of bones bled dry.

DEAN: Bled dry? God bless my soul,
young man, I'm not a ghoul!
I speak with fair intent.
For your own betterment,
for your future career,
you must knock on the right door.

BRAND: Dean, when the cock crowed thrice
it sounded like your voice.
Do you suppose that I'll
deny . . . ?

DEAN: Who said 'denial'?
Eschew every risk.
That's not much to ask.

BRAND: 'The fear of strife, the greed for gain,
Upon thy brow the mark of Cain,
Emblazoned there when thou did smite
Innocent Abel in thy heart.'

DEAN [*aside*]:
Far too familiar!
Why won't he call me 'sir'?
       [*Aloud*]
I fear that we must cut
short our little debate.
To sum up what's been said:
you can't hope to succeed
unless you come to terms
with the mood of the times.
It's just as the Mayor says –
this nation's changed its ways,
and soft and soothing words
prevail, and blunted swords.
Why, even our poets
take care, now, to carol
their praise of the moral,
the civil, pursuits.
'More mediocrity',
that's now the nation's cry.
'It's better to be led,
citizens, than to lead!'

BRAND: Dear God, to go from here!

DEAN: One finds one's proper sphere,
all in good time. Be calm,
acquire a uniform
in keeping with the age. A

drill-sergeant or drum-major
drumming up church parades,
the Eucharistic squads,
a pastor marching his
recruits to Paradise.
A man can do things blind-
fold, my young friend,
if he's a believer.
Well, well, think it over.
There's a lot to be done.
I really must rehearse
my forthcoming address
to find the correct tone
and pitch. By the way, Brand,
by the way, I intend
to take as my main theme
'Spirit versus Flesh' – you know –
Dualism, the tragic flaw,
it's all here. Have I time
for a quick – ah – repast?

> [*Exit.* BRAND *stands for a moment as if paralysed by his own thoughts.*]

BRAND: Like Mammon's trumpet-blast
taunting my sacrifice,
making the clouds disperse,
showing me the depraved
spirits that I served,
how hideously that creature 'spake'
the truth, though never for truth's sake.
This bitter place has drained my blood
and buried all my earthly good
and ruined all my great design
and nothing that was mine is mine
except the soul that I withhold
from the smooth demons of the world.
The holy dove has not descended.
If I could find once more on earth
faithfulness answering my faith,

and know that solitude had ended . . .

[EINAR, *pale, emaciated, dressed in black, comes along
the road and stops as he sees* BRAND.]

Einar!

EINAR: That is my name.

BRAND: Einar, it's like a dream!
I prayed I might find one
person not made of stone.
Let me embrace you!

EINAR: Please
refrain. I've reached my haven.

BRAND: You reject my embrace?
So you've still not forgiven?

EINAR: What was there to forgive?
Reprobate that you are,
I know you for a mere
instrument of God's love
to me, His child of grace.

BRAND: Harsh words.

EINAR: Pure words of peace
that we, the blessèd, learn
when our souls are reborn.

BRAND: Strange – for wild rumour said
that you'd gone to the bad –

EINAR: But true! I went astray
lured by the world's display,
believing its false gauds,
with pride in my own words,
my songs as they were called.
How little they availed!
But, God be praised, He broke
my strength to draw me back.
He thrust me down: I sank
into His mire; I drank
brandy and took to cards.

BRAND: You call such tricks the Lord's?

EINAR: He tested my poor worth
with sickness unto death;

and I was stripped of all
I had. In hospital,
in my delirium,
I saw swarm upon swarm
of monstrous bloated flies.
Then, after my release,
I met - and not by chance,
by divine providence –
three sisters, three pure souls
who freed me from the toils
of sin, and from the world.
And I became a child
of grace. God's ways with us
are strange; and various
are the paths we must tread
to our doom or reward.

BRAND: Various indeed! And then?

EINAR: I sought my brother-man,
brought him to God. At first,
as an evangelist,
I plucked many a soul
from fiery alcohol
till I began to dread
the old pull that it had.
So I'm joining a mission
for Bible propagation
among the heathen.

BRAND: Where?

EINAR: Far enough from here –
the Negroes, so I'm told –
Caudates I think they're called.

BRAND: Look, Einar, won't you stay,
at least for today,
just for the festival?

EINAR: No. I bid you farewell.

BRAND: Has nothing, then, remained;
no glad or grieving thought,
no tenderness of heart,

    no warmth of any kind?
EINAR: Ah, the young female who
    enticed me, to my woe,
    before faith made me pure!
    Well, what became of her?
BRAND: Agnes became my wife.
    You hadn't heard? Our life
    knew grief as well as joy.
EINAR: That doesn't signify.
BRAND: We were blessed with a son,
    our only child. He soon
    died, though, our little boy.
EINAR: That doesn't signify.
BRAND: And then Agnes died.
    Close by my church I laid
    them both to rest. Now say,
    'That doesn't signify'!
EINAR: Such things mean nothing. Tell
    me: what of her state of soul?
BRAND: She fell asleep with utter faith
    in new life dawning after death;
    by love and gratitude possessed
    and strength of will, until the last
    breath of her being. Thus she died:
    trusting the great things that abide.
EINAR: Vaingloriousness and sham
    piety to cover shame!
    What assurances did
    she have?
BRAND: Firm faith in God;
    rock-firm!
EINAR: That won't avail
    her now. She's damned.
BRAND [*calmly*]:
                        You fool.
EINAR: Both reprobate; both damned;
    you – and she whom you named.
BRAND: You dare say that? You who were

sprawled in corruption's mire?

EINAR: But newly risen without stain!
I was immersed in the divine
wash-tub; pounded by the dolly-
stick of His anger! I was wholly
cleansed on the scrubbing-board of our
redemption, by the soap of prayer!

BRAND: Soap of prayer? Spit it out!

EINAR: I am pure heavenly wheat;
and you, chaff for the fire.
I can smell sulphur here.
I see the devil's horns.

[*Exit.* BRAND *looks after him for a few moments; then
suddenly his eyes light up.*]

BRAND [*exclaiming*]:
And I have burst the chains
you bound me with! I shrug
them off. From now on I
fight under my own flag
whether or not any
man chooses to follow.

MAYOR [*entering hurriedly*]:
Brand! Be a good fellow
and hurry up. It's late
and they're shouting, 'Why wait?'
and 'Start the procession!',
'We want Pastor Brand!',
and so on, in a fashion
that's most unseemly. They're
getting out of hand.

BRAND: Then let them, Mister Mayor,
let them; for here I stay;
and your rabble can shout,
'Hosannah' or 'Crucify'
just as they please. I'll not
betray myself again
for you, or any man
who jumps when you nod.

MAYOR [*shouting*]:
   Keep back, keep to the road!
      [*More quietly*]
   My dear Pastor, I urge
   you, wield the scourge,
   exert your influence
   as a man of the cloth!
   We'll be trampled to death!
   Too late! There goes the fence!
      [*The* CROWD *surges in and breaks in wild disorder
      through the festive procession towards the church.*]

VOICES FROM THE CROWD: Pastor, give us a sign!
   Show us the New Zion!

DEAN [*overrun by the mob*]:
   Use your authority!

MAYOR: They won't listen to me!

SCHOOLMASTER: Pastor, for pity's sake,
   don't just stand there. Is this
   the truth you promised us?
   Make them see reason. Talk
   to them; turn their minds
   to higher things!

BRAND: Fresh winds,
   fresh winds of change are blowing,
   purging and renewing!
      [*Shouts to the* CROWD]
   Here's where the roads divide;
   here you must turn aside
   out of the old rut,
   to seek the absolute,
   God's one true dwelling place!

AN OFFICIAL: He's mad!

A CLERIC: It's a disgrace!

BRAND: *I was* mad. I believed
   that even you still served
   the mighty God of truth.
   I set foot on the path
   that led to compromise.

I played your petty games;
I walked as you walk;
I talked in your terms.
So, my church was too small.
So, I thought I'd amaze
God Himself with the bulk
of His new citadel.
In my pride I forgot
that the words 'all or nothing'
mean what they say. The trumpet
of His judgement has shrilled
above this place. I'm filled
with dread and self-loathing,
as David stood accurst
for an unholy lust.
But this much is certain:
the riches of Satan
are our self-betrayals,
are our perjured souls.

VOICES [*in mounting excitement*]:
He's right! We must have been
blind! Cast them out! Swine!

BRAND: 'Close behind thee squats the Fiend.
In his meshes thou art bound.
By his wiles thou art possessed,
all thy hardihood laid waste,
made a stranger to thyself,
drowned in desolation's gulf.'
You who go to church to stuff
your souls with solemn fustian,
tell me: was that spiced enough?
Or did it seem un-Christian?
You love the organ and the bells;
love to hear a well-rehearsed
sermon full of little thrills,
trills of dogma nicely phrased,
sacred torrents in full spate,
cascades of the speaker's art.

MAYOR [*aside*]:
    That's the Dean's voice, loud and clear.
DEAN [*aside*]:
    Surely he must mean the Mayor.
BRAND: The candles in the holy place,
    the vestments and the carapace
    of piety, that's all you ask:
    pantomimes to send you home
    deafened, surfeited, and dumb,
    fitted for the daily task,
    glad to put your souls away
    in camphor with your Sunday best,
    ready for the next day of rest,
    unready for the Judgement Day.
DEAN: Citizens, eschew that man!
    He's not a Christian. Well, I mean,
    he spurns our faith!
BRAND: You speak of faith?
    That's long since vanished from the earth.
    It vanished when man lost his soul.
    It doesn't answer when you call.
    Show me the man who has not cast
    spiritual treasure in the dust
    and ashes of a wasted life.
    Jigging to the scrawny fife,
    clown and cripple show their legs,
    dance themselves into the muck
    of blasphemy before the Ark,
    all drained and bitter as the dregs.
    It's reckoning time: 'Repent! repent!'
    Time for amendment and for cant.
    Hey presto, penitence and prayer!
    Hey presto, 'Save us from despair!'
    What a sick parade of wretches
    lurching towards Heaven on crutches,
    maimed in body and in soul,
    besieging mercy's citadel!
    Yet listen to the voice of God:

'Give me now thy precious blood,
give to me of thy pure spirit.
Thou art chosen to inherit.
Be then as a little child:
be the child within the man;
flesh and spirit undefiled,
enter into thy domain.'
MAYOR: Unlock the church, then.
VOICES [*crying out as if in anguish*]:

> No! No!

Pastor, tell us what to do!
BRAND: Jerusalem's temple, seek it out,
that altar blazing on the height.
It is the earth on which we stand,
the world of Adam reordained.
Let faith be life; your daily work
like David's dance before the Ark.
Then truth and dogma shall be one,
and body shall belong to soul,
and soul embody the divine,
and majesty shall be the small
child's wonder at the Christmas game;
shall be the starlight through the storm.
> [*There is a movement, as of a storm, among the* CROWD;
> *some shrink back; most gather closely round* BRAND.]
VOICES: He brings us light! Drives out the dark!
DEAN: Scoundrel! Seducer of Christ's flock!
Desist at once, d'you hear?
Have him arrested, Mayor!
MAYOR: Not I! I'd be a fool
to fight with a mad bull.
Let him bellow and snort.
Let him tire himself out.
BRAND: Far from this hideous place,
from Pilate, from Caiaphas,
still shines the promised land
and the unfinished quest.
Here I'm no longer priest.

Snatch this key from my hand
if you dare.
     [*Throws it into the river*]
          I revoke
my covenant. I take
back from you each gift
I ever gave. What's left
is all yours, child-of-dirt,
feeble-thought, faint-heart!

MAYOR [*aside*]:
There goes his Knight's Grand Cross.

DEAN [*aside*]:
There goes his diocese.

BRAND: You who are still young,
with strength to stay the course,
awake from the dead sleep
of shame and compromise
and dust and squalor.
Listen to the air sing
over summit and steep.
Arise, arise, and learn
what it is to be men
possessed of true valour
in a holy war!

A VOICE: Lead on, Pastor, we'll
follow you anywhere!

BRAND: Follow, then, those who will!
March away across the frozen
crests, across that sea of snow,
to valleys waiting for the thaw;
rouse the captives in their prison,
topple Dagon at his feast;
by your strength and your example
be the builders of the temple,
make of every man a priest!

    [*The* CROWD, *which includes the* SEXTON *and the*
    SCHOOLMASTER, *surges round him.* BRAND *is*
    raised aloft on the men's shoulders.]

VOICES: Such visions! Ah, such prophecies!
    Like the sun to our eyes!
DEAN [*as they begin to leave*]:
    Visions? Visions? You're blind!
    Led astray by the Fiend!
MAYOR: You hear what the Dean says!
    Stay put in the parish;
    enjoy the good life;
    avoid stormy seas,
    good people, or perish.
    You fools, are you deaf?
A VOICE: Our lives are now the Lord's!
MAYOR: You wait! You'll eat your words!
ANOTHER VOICE: The Israelites were given
    manna from Heaven!
MAYOR [*shaking his fist at* BRAND]:
    Disgraceful! But you'll pay
    for this, come reckoning day!
DEAN: The scoundrel! O my sheep,
    my stipend! I could weep.
MAYOR: They haven't gone far yet.
    They'll soon begin to bleat.
    [*He follows them.*]
DEAN: Hey! Where are you going?
    What on earth's the Mayor doing?
    Is he out of his mind?
    This stirs up my old blood!
    I'll follow them; by God,
    I'll not be left behind.
    [*Exit.*]

★

At the highest pasture of the village. The landscape rises in the background and turns into vast, desolate mountain heights. It is raining. BRAND, *followed by the crowd — men, women and children — comes over the slopes.*

    BRAND: Look up, look far and high!
    Fare forward to your spirits' home,

you men-of-God! Your dead selves lie
behind you in the valley gloom.

A MAN: My old dad, he's worn out.

ANOTHER MAN: Gi'e us summat to eat.

A WOMAN: And we're that parched wi' thirst.

BRAND: On, on, to the crest!

SCHOOLMASTER: But which way?

BRAND: Any road
that gets us there is good.

SEXTON: The Ice Church is up there.

ANOTHER WOMAN: Eh, but my feet are sore.

BRAND: The steep way's the shortest.
Fight! When you've fought, rest.

SCHOOLMASTER: Give them strength; their courage fails!

VOICES: Miracles, we want miracles!

BRAND: You want! You want! The mark
of slavery's deep in you yet!
You want profit without sweat.
Press forward; or fall, back-
sliding into the grave.

SCHOOLMASTER: He's right . . . We must be brave.
We shall have our reward.

BRAND: As surely as the Lord
turns on us His just gaze!

VOICES: Hear him! He prophesies!
Pastor, will the fight be hot
and bloody? Oh, I hope it's not.
What's my share when we've won?
Don't take my only son.

SEXTON: Will the victory be ours
by Tuesday, d'you suppose?

BRAND [looking around the CROWD, bewildered]:
What is it? What do you want?

SEXTON: We want the full account.
First: how long will it last?
Second: what will it cost?
Third: what's the profit for us?

BRAND: So that's the question!

SCHOOLMASTER: Yes,
> Pastor. We want the truth,
> 'straight from the horse's mouth'.

BRAND: How long will the strife last?
> Till you have sacrificed
> all your earthly good,
> every last farthing;
> till you have understood
> what the words 'all or nothing'
> truly mean; till you control
> your own strength, your own soul.
> What will your losses be?
> Ancient idolatry,
> and servitude that shines
> weighed down with golden chains
> and deep pillows of sloth,
> your thraldom to earth.
> What will the victor's wreath
> be? It will be faith
> raised up; it will be joy
> in sacrifice; integrity
> of the soul; everyman's
> triumph, his crown of thorns!

VOICES [*furiously*]:
> Judas! We've been betrayed!

BRAND: I have kept my word!

A VOICE: You promised victories –
> but talk of sacrifice,
> and ask us to lay down
> our lives for those unborn.

BRAND: To get to Canaan we must pass
> like Moses through the wilderness.
> All who keep faith shall walk this road
> as victors chosen of the Lord.

SEXTON: Here's a fine to-do.
> We'll never dare to show
> our heads.

SCHOOLMASTER: We can't go home,

Sexton, think of the shame.

SEXTON: We can't go on. We're stuck,
   for certain-sure.

VOICES: Turn back!
   Hey! stone him, lads! Curse
   him!

SCHOOLMASTER:
      'Thou shalt not murder.'
   And our plight would be far worse
   without a leader.

A WOMAN [*pointing back down the path*]:
   Mercy – the Dean – it's *him*!

SCHOOLMASTER: Please try to stay calm!
      [*The* DEAN *arrives, followed by a few of those who had
      stayed behind.*]

DEAN: O my flock,
   hear your old shepherd speak!

SCHOOLMASTER [*to the* CROWD]:
   Too late, too late. We'd best
   follow the Pastor now.

DEAN: You plunge knives in my breast,
   you set thorns on my brow!

BRAND: Dean, Dean, you've tortured souls
   year in, year out.

DEAN: O heed
   him not, my friends. He's fed
   you dreams and wicked tales.

A VOICE: Ay, that he has!

DEAN: The Church
   is ready to forgive
   those who show true remorse.
   Look deep in your own hearts
   and surely you'll perceive
   the black and hellish arts
   you're caught with.

VOICES: Why, of course!
   We were deceived! The wretch!

DEAN: What weapons can the humble wield

146

upon the heroes' battlefield?
And how, I wonder, would you fare,
helpless between the wolf and bear,
between the eagle and the hawk?
The strong prey on the weak,
and you are weak, my lambs.
Go back to your homes.

A VOICE: True! Everything he says!

SEXTON: We locked the village doors
and threw away our keys.
There's nothing left that's ours.

SCHOOLMASTER: For my part, I'm prepared
to put in a good word
or two for the priest.
We slept in the past.
He opened our eyes
to a world of old lies;
brought life where there was none.
I say we've been reborn!

DEAN: Such feelings will soon pass.
You'll fold to the old crease,
you'll plod down the old rut,
I can promise you that.

BRAND: Choose — all of you!

VOICES: We want —
we want to go back! We can't!
Move forward! To the crest!

MAYOR [arrives, running]:
What luck! Found you at last!
Must catch my breath . . .

A WOMAN: Sir, please
don't take it out on us,
we never meant no harm.

MAYOR: Be quiet . . . What a climb!
Listen to me, you'll all
be rich by nightfall!

VOICES: Rich by nightfall, he says!

MAYOR: A mighty shoal of fish

out there in the fjord –
millions – all yours to take –
you'll find they jump aboard –
I've never seen the like
in all my born days!
It's new life for the parish.
Come home with me, good folk!
This is no time for talk!

BRAND: Choose between God and Mammon!

MAYOR: Don't heed him. Use your common
sense!

DEAN: It's an oracle
from Heaven; a miracle
beyond your wildest dreams,
eh children, eh my lambs?

BRAND: If you yield now, you're lost.

A VOICE: Fish in the fjord – the most
there's ever been!

MAYOR: Billions!

DEAN: Bread for your little ones,
gold coins in your pockets.

MAYOR: Don't question luck; it's
high time for you to learn
what things we leave alone
and where we stake our claim.
Fare forth, my friends, bring home
the bounty of the deep.
No need for blood and sweat,
no need at all. Let's keep
sacrifice out of it.

BRAND: Sacrifice is written in words
of fire, blazing high in the clouds!

DEAN: It depends how you feel
of course. Any fine Sunday I'll
be happy to extol
sacrifice to one and all.

MAYOR: Yes, *some* fine day, eh Dean?

SEXTON [*to* DEAN]:

Look, sir . . . you'll keep me on?

SCHOOLMASTER [*to* DEAN]:

You'll not have me dismissed
(Heaven forbid) from my post?

DEAN [*quietly*]:

Well, again, that depends –
a quiet word with your friends . . .
Make the crowd walk *our* way,
then, no doubt, leniency . . .
you understand? h'm? h'm? . . .

MAYOR: Come on, we're wasting time!

SEXTON: I'm off to find my boat.

A VOICE: The Pastor . . . what about?

SEXTON: Argh! Let him rot, the fool . . .

SCHOOLMASTER: 'Tis the Lord's will, the Lord's will.

MAYOR: Act as God's law requires
with all such thieves and liars.

VOICES: He lied to us! He lied
to us!

DEAN: Nothing but lies.
If you ask me, he's
not even qualified!

VOICES: The nerve! What *has* he got?

MAYOR: The Order of the Boot!

SEXTON: That fellow's a wrong
'un; I've said so all along!

DEAN: He cursed his dear mother
as she lay at death's door,
refused her communion.

MAYOR: He killed his own son.

SEXTON: He broke his poor wife's heart.

A WOMAN: Men like that should be shot.

DEAN: Cruel father, cruel spouse!
What, I ask, could be worse?

VOICES: He pulled down the old church,
that's worse! Ay, tore it down!
Locked us out of the new 'un.

MAYOR: The scoundrel stole my plan,

my gift to the insane.
BRAND: That gift? It's yours, Mayor;
all yours: madness, despair!
VOICES: Flay him! Throttle him! Shut
his mouth! Out! Out!
[*Bellowing*]
Out! Out! Out! Out!
[BRAND *is driven and stoned across the wastelands.*
Then, gradually, his pursuers return.]
DEAN: My children, O my lambs,
return to your own homes!
Gaze with repentant eyes
on God, all-good, all-wise.
He'll not eat you. He'll
not pack you off to Hell.
You'll find the government
extremely tolerant;
the justices of the peace
will fold you in their embrace
while I, in my own right,
exude sweetness and light.
MAYOR: We're ready to appoint –
(by 'we', of course, I mean
myself and the Dean) –
a regional committee
to deal with each complaint
in peace and charity:
a clergyman or two,
the Schoolmaster, he'll do;
the Sexton; plus a couple
more, two sturdy sons of toil
picked out from the people
to sit with their betters.
We'll give you all you want,
progress, enlightenment,
self-help? free thought? We'll
knock off your fetters!
DEAN: Why, yes. We'll ease your load,

just as you've lightened mine
(I can rest easy again!)
so rejoice and be glad.
In short, get back to work.
Good fishing, and good luck!

SEXTON: True Christians both, as fine
as ever I've seen!

A VOICE: Oh yes! They know what's right.

SEXTON: They don't tell you to 'fight,
fight till you drop'!

SCHOOLMASTER: You feel those two can cope
with more than mere pieties.
They know what life is.

[*The* CROWD *begins to move down the slopes.*]

DEAN [*to* MAYOR]:
Well, that's improved the tone,
all the harm's been undone
and reaction's restored,
praise be to the Lord!

MAYOR: And who, may I inquire,
came and put out the fire?
Who else but yours truly!

DEAN: Tch, Mayor, that's a wholly
uncalled-for remark!
'Twas the Lord's handiwork.

MAYOR: You think so?

DEAN: Yes, that shoal
in the fjord . . .

MAYOR: That wasn't *real.*

DEAN: You uttered an untruth?

MAYOR: I just opened my mouth –
hey Bingo – out it came!
Don't tell me that's a crime.

DEAN: Such sleights may be allowed,
my son, in time of need.

MAYOR: In dire emergencies
what are a few white lies?

DEAN: I'm neither prig nor prude.

[*Looks across the barren wastes*]
Good heavens above! Look there –
isn't that our friend
limping over the ground?
MAYOR: Like a lost warrior
seeking his lost crusade.
DEAN: And trudging close behind –
MAYOR: Poor Gerd, I do declare!
Well, they're two of a kind.
DEAN [*jestingly*]:
He'll need an epitaph.
How's this for a laugh?
'Here lies a pure young pastor.
He was a pure disaster.
He's left all that he had,
one convert, and she's mad.'
MAYOR [*with his finger on his nose*]:
But, come to think of it,
his treatment's not been quite –
how can I put it – *fair.*
DEAN [*shrugging*]:
Vox populi, vox Dei, Mayor!
[*Exeunt.*]

★

Out on the great open heights. The storm is gathering strength and driving the clouds, low and heavy, over the snowy wastes; black pinnacles and peaks now and then appear and are again blurred by the mist. BRAND *comes, bruised and bleeding, across the heights.*

BRAND [*stopping and looking back*]:
A thousand followers. And not one
followed me here. Where have they gone,
then, the struggle and all the great
yearning to reach the farthest height?
Their pitiful vainglorious dream
of sacrifice! Have they no shame;
or do they think Christ Crucified

made all sins decent when He died?
We battle for our souls. I knew
fear in my time; watched it; it grew;
it moved as I moved, as I tried
to find my heart a place to hide.
'The trolls are dead; and it is not
night; and the sun grows round and hot
above the fjord in its round dance,
in pure midsummer radiance.'
How fearful, then, when I awoke
from vividness into the shock
of dark where men moved shadowy
like ghosts beside the frozen sea;
sad mockeries of that old king
of Norway, his weird suffering,
locked in his grief for his dead queen,
her heartbeats locked inside his brain.
You cannot bury death in dreams
of life; and nothing else redeems
death from itself but life-in-death,
the live seed buried in the earth.
But now this hideous age ordains
blood and iron (for as few pains
as possible). Some flinch. And some
go in good faith to fight the storm.
The best go. The worst wring their hands,
groaning, 'The age, the age demands!'
Worse times, worse visions, they are here
already: locust swarms of fear,
war clouds and clouds of industry
drawing their filth across the sky.
Deep down, the soulless dwarfs who made
an empire quarrying men's greed
set free the stony-fettered ore
the better to constrain its power.
They labour so, grow old and die
enslaved by their own mastery;
the clicking water of the mine

cold requiem when they are gone!
Truth is not seen or else is seen
too late, ruins where storms have been.
A nation smug amid the gloom
savours its penitential psalm:
'Not for us His cup was drained,
not for us the kiss that burned,
not for us the thorny crown
rooted in His blood that ran.
Not for us, O not for us
to seek salvation at His Cross.
For us only the whip that rakes
fresh scars across our spineless backs!'

> [*He throws himself down in the snow and covers his face
> with his hands. After some moments he looks up.*]

Am I now waking from a sleep
of sickness, from some demon's grip?
Did I hear once, through the world's din,
the song of the soul's origin?

CHORUS OF SPIRITS: God is God and man can never
be like Him. You thing of dust,
defy Him; be His abject lover;
either way your soul is lost!

BRAND: I have been dispossessed by God;
God has withdrawn from His own Word;
His clouds of wrath blot out the sun;
accursèd is the altar-stone.

CHORUS: God is God and *is* for ever.
You shall live your life of death,
self-inspiring self-deceiver,
cheated by your dying breath.

BRAND: I sacrificed my wife, my child,
and all my comfort in this world,
and yet the serpent was not slain!
And was my sacrifice my sin?

CHORUS: God is God. He grants no favour,
no return for life that's past.
All your sacrificial savour

smells like any carnal feast.

BRAND [*beginning to weep quietly*]:
Agnes, my wife; and oh, my son,
my son, Alf – what have I done,
and why? And do you – poor ghosts –
cling together in these weeping mists?

[BRAND *looks up; an area of growing light opens and
spreads itself in the mist; the form of a woman stands
there, dressed in light colours, with a cloak over her shoulders. It is* AGNES.]

AGNES: Look at me, Brand.

BRAND: Love! Is it you?

AGNES: Yes, I am Agnes.

BRAND: The child, too,
is he . . . ?

AGNES: He is safe and sound.
He misses you. No, Brand!
Stay where you are. The stream
divides us now.

BRAND: A dream!

AGNES: No dream.
I stay as long as you desire.

BRAND: For ever, then!

AGNES: Brand, all my care
has been for you. When you were filled
with frantic rage against the world
I tried to calm you. I was beside
you, even though you dreamed I died.

BRAND: You are alive!

AGNES: And you shall live
once more in what you have.
I've said, the child is well;
he's with your mother. Oh how tall
he's grown! The church still stands
just as it always stood. Your friends
are watching for the day
of your return. Love, come away!
Surely the good days wait for us!

BRAND: It *is* a dream.

AGNES: Refuse
   these gifts of life? Be lost
   for ever in a mist?
   Love, love, come and be healed.

BRAND: I still
   know, despite all, that my own will
   is my salvation, my true peace.
   You plead for a false sacrifice.

AGNES: Brand, *I* am your salvation now!
   Our friend, the old doctor, saw
   deep, deep into your soul
   where you hid from us all,
   enraptured by your cruel visions.
   He called you a man of dark passions.
   'Most passionate for each extreme.
   He must will himself to be calm,'
   he said, 'teach his heart a new tune.
   "All or nothing" is good for no one.'

BRAND [*turning away*]:
   Is this true?

AGNES: As true as I live;
   true as your way of death. O love,
   all that I did was for your good!

BRAND: *That* you have never understood!
   You condemn me. Your care betrays
   me, and insinuates old ways.
   You have betrayed us both. A sword
   gleams between us, and always would!

AGNES: Be gentle, Brand. In my embrace
   the anguish and the fearful price
   can be forgotten. No more pain . . .

BRAND: Old wounds won't bleed again.
   Anguish of dreams is dead.
   Life's horror comes instead.
   Follow me, Agnes.

AGNES: But the child,
   Brand!

BRAND: Leave him!

AGNES: No! No wild
nightmares of riding at your back
like a dead woman wide awake!

BRAND: All or nothing. Truth, not lies.
My vision, not your fantasies!

AGNES: The seraph with the sword of flame,
remember, Brand? And Adam's doom,
remember? And the dread abyss
before the gate? You shall not pass
into your self-willed paradise!

BRAND: God left one last approach for us:
the way of longing!

> [AGNES *disappears as in a thunderclap; the mist rolls in
> over the place where she stood; there is a sharp and
> penetrating cry, as from one fleeing.*]

AGNES: Die, Brand, die!
All life disowns your destiny!

BRAND [*standing for a few moments as if stunned*]:
It vanished so suddenly.
Cheated of what it came to seek —
my soul's blood on its claws and beak —
it screamed for its lost prey.
Was *that* the ghost of compromise?

GERD [*entering, carrying a rifle*]:
The hawk! Did you see him?

BRAND: This time,
yes, there was a hawk.
It came so very close.

GERD: Which way has he flown? Quick,
tell me! I'll follow him.

BRAND: Shape-shifter that it is, sometimes
it vanishes. Sometimes it looms
large and terrible. We imagine
it is dead; then, at the margin
of vision, watch it reappear,
playing give-and-take with the wild air.

GERD: See what I have!

BRAND: A bullet?

GERD: Made of pure silver. I stole it
   from a huntsman. They say it works
   wonders against demons.

BRAND: And hawks?
   Real phantom-hawks?

GERD: Who knows?

BRAND: Well, aim
   to kill.

        [*He starts to leave.*]

GERD: Hey, preacher-man, you're lame!
   Why are you lame?

BRAND: My own
   people – the people – scourged and stoned
   me; hunted me down.

GERD: Blood's pouring from your face;
   and your clothes are stained.

BRAND: Everything and everyone –

GERD: Your voice,
   it's rasping like dead leaves . . .

BRAND: Betrayed –
   I have been betrayed!

GERD [*looking at him, wide-eyed*]:
               I know
   who you are; I know you now!
   You're not the preacher, not a bit
   like him. He makes me spit.
   You're some great man!

BRAND: I dreamed so indeed.
   Was I mad?

GERD: Show me your hands.
   It's true, it's true! . . . those wounds!
   Oh, and your lovely head,
   all snagged and smeary from the thorn!
   Dear saviour-man, why aren't you dead,
   like in the stories I was told?
   Long, long ago, and far away,
   a little gypsy-boy was born;

and he was king of all the world,
and so they killed him on a cross.
It was my father told me this.
Why did he tell me such a lie?
O Saviour, let me kiss your feet!

BRAND: Out of my sight!

GERD: Your blood can save us all!

BRAND: Not even my own soul.

GERD: I'm canny; I can shoot;
　　　you told me, 'Aim to kill.'
　　　I can! I can do it!

BRAND [shaking his head]:
　　　Child, let them be: weak, struggling men.
　　　Let them strive and stumble on
　　　until they fall.

GERD:　　　　　　You'll never fall.
　　　For on your head's the thorny crown;
　　　and in your hands the prints of nails
　　　bear witness that you're God's dear Son.

BRAND: I am the meanest thing that crawls.

GERD [looking upward; the clouds are breaking]:
　　　Do you see where we are?

BRAND: I see the mountain and the stair,
　　　clear through the mist; the pure ascent,
　　　the void that is the firmament.
　　　It is the Ice Church!

GERD [uttering a wild cry]:
　　　　　　　　　　Yes! now you come!

BRAND [starting to weep]:
　　　Redeemer, when I called Your name,
　　　prayed for the comfort of Your arm,
　　　You passed close by and never heard.
　　　Dear name, the ghost of an old word . . .
　　　Redeemer, look, I try to touch
　　　Your white robe, but I cannot reach.
　　　Sinners whose tears have stained its hem
　　　put all my agony to shame.

GERD [*pale*]:
Oh now the priest-of-ice
is melting; rags and tatters drop
from his glacier cope;
the tears pour down his face.
The ice in my own brain
melts to a gentle rain
and all that freezing fire
is gone. You would not weep before.
Why? Why?

BRAND [*radiant and as if reborn*]:
                    Narrow was my path,
straitened between wrath and wrath.
My own heart was the Sinai slate
on which the hand of God could write.
Before this hour, until this place,
I knew no other power, no grace,
beyond my own unyielding will.
But now the sunshine and the thaw.
And life shall be my song. Here, now,
I am released, and kneel!

GERD [*looking upward and speaking slowly and fearfully*]:
Silver to silver, steel to flesh
of ice where those great feathers thresh:
look how he beats against the rock.
Now, silver bullet, flash and strike!
    [*She puts the rifle to her shoulder and fires. A hollow
    booming, as of a roll of thunder, sounds from high up the
    mountain face.*]

BRAND: What have you done?

GERD: That strange white bird,
he screamed; he screamed as I fired!
Silver-white ice-dove, do you cry
with terror now? Ah, the beauty!
He's plunging down, he's scattering
whirlwinds of feathers from each wing;
a mountain whirling like a swarm
of feathery snow. And now that scream,

nearer, nearer . . . Oh the noise, the noise!

[*She throws herself down in the snow.*]

BRAND [*shrinking under the approaching avalanche and crying out*]:   Tell
me, O God, even as Your heavens fall
on me: what makes retribution
flesh of our flesh? Why is salvation
rooted so blindly in Your Cross?
Why is man's own proud will his curse?
Answer! What do we die to prove?
Answer!

[*The avalanche buries him. The whole valley is filled.*]

A VOICE [*calling through the noise of thunder*]:
He is the God of Love.

READ MORE IN PENGUIN

In every corner of the world, on every subject under the sun, Penguin represents quality and variety – the very best in publishing today.

For complete information about books available from Penguin – including Puffins, Penguin Classics and Arkana – and how to order them, write to us at the appropriate address below. Please note that for copyright reasons the selection of books varies from country to country.

In the United Kingdom: Please write to *Dept. EP, Penguin Books Ltd, Bath Road, Harmondsworth, West Drayton, Middlesex UB7 0DA*

In the United States: Please write to *Consumer Sales, Penguin USA, P.O. Box 999, Dept. 17109, Bergenfield, New Jersey 07621-0120.* VISA and MasterCard holders call 1-800-253-6476 to order Penguin titles

In Canada: Please write to *Penguin Books Canada Ltd, 10 Alcorn Avenue, Suite 300, Toronto, Ontario M4V 3B2*

In Australia: Please write to *Penguin Books Australia Ltd, P.O. Box 257, Ringwood, Victoria 3134*

In New Zealand: Please write to *Penguin Books (NZ) Ltd, Private Bag 102902, North Shore Mail Centre, Auckland 10*

In India: Please write to *Penguin Books India Pvt Ltd, 706 Eros Apartments, 56 Nehru Place, New Delhi 110 019*

In the Netherlands: Please write to *Penguin Books Netherlands bv, Postbus 3507, NL-1001 AH Amsterdam*

In Germany: Please write to *Penguin Books Deutschland GmbH, Metzlerstrasse 26, 60594 Frankfurt am Main*

In Spain: Please write to *Penguin Books S. A., Bravo Murillo 19, 1° B, 28015 Madrid*

In Italy: Please write to *Penguin Italia s.r.l., Via Felice Casati 20, I–20124 Milano*

In France: Please write to *Penguin France S. A., 17 rue Lejeune, F–31000 Toulouse*

In Japan: Please write to *Penguin Books Japan, Ishikiribashi Building, 2–5–4, Suido, Bunkyo-ku, Tokyo 112*

In Greece: Please write to *Penguin Hellas Ltd, Dimocritou 3, GR–106 71 Athens*

In South Africa: Please write to *Longman Penguin Southern Africa (Pty) Ltd, Private Bag X08, Bertsham 2013*